A NILE ANTHOLOGY

A NILE ANTHOLOGY

Travel Writing through the Centuries

Edited by
Deborah Manley
and Sahar Abdel-Hakim

With illustrations from
The Nile Boat by W.H. Bartlett

The American University in Cairo Press
Cairo New York

The illustrations are taken from W.H. Bartlett, *The Nile Boat or Glimpses of the Land of Egypt*. London: Arthur Hall, 1849. Courtesy of the Rare Books and Special Collections Library of the American University in Cairo.

The editors and publisher are grateful to the following for permission to use material in this book: Methuen Publishing Ltd. for the excerpt from H.V. Morton's *Through Lands of the Bible* (© Marion Wasdell and Brian de Villiers); The Random House Group Ltd. for the excerpt from *The Travels of Ibn Jubayr*, translated by R.J.C. Broadhurst and published by Jonathan Cape.

113 Sharia Kasr el Aini, Cairo, Egypt
420 Fifth Avenue, New York, NY 10018
www.aucpress.com

Exclusive distribution outside Egypt and North America by I.B.Tauris & Co Ltd., 6 Salem Road, London, W2 4BU

Dar el Kutub No. 25665/14
ISBN 978 977 416 732 2

Dar el Kutub Cataloging-in-Publication Data

Manley, Deborah
A Nile Anthology: Two hundred years of travel writing/ Deborah Manley and Sahar Abdel Hakim—Cairo: The American University in Cairo Press, 2015.
p. cm.
ISBN 978 977 416 732 2
Egypt—History—20th Century
I Abd El Hakim, Sahar (Jt auth.)
962

1 2 3 4 5 19 18 17 16 15

Project editor: Bonnie McGinty
Designed by Fatiha Bouzidi
Printed in the United States of America

Contents

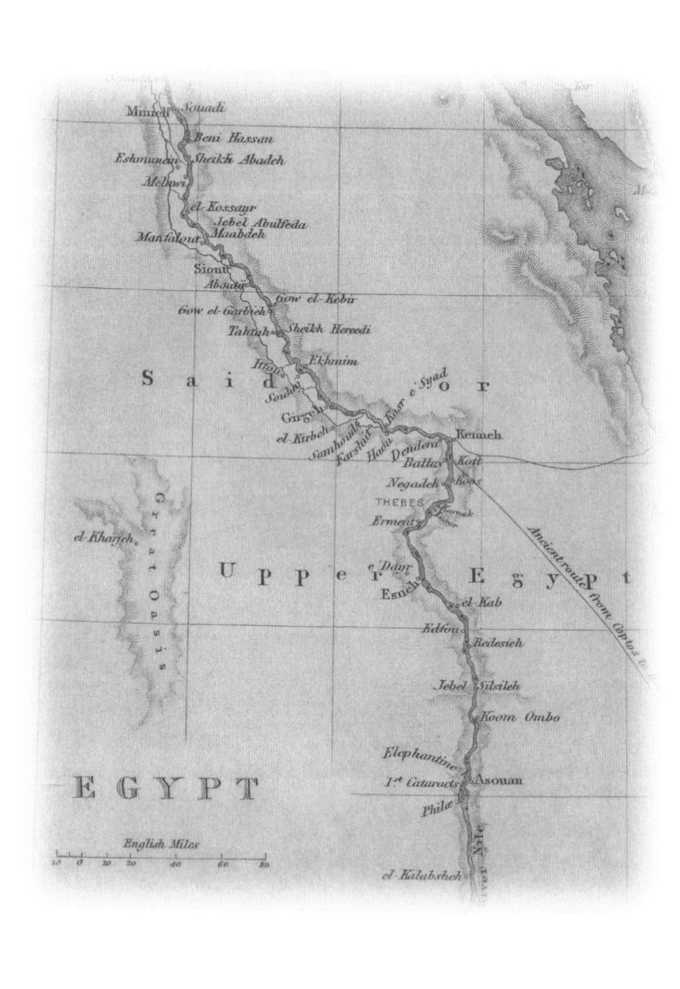

Minieh
Souadi
Beni Hassan
Eshmunein
Sheikh Abadeh
Melawi
el-Kossayr
Jebel Abulfeda
Manfalout
Maabdeh
Siout
Abouti
Gow el-Kebir
Gow el-Garbieh
Tahtah
Sheikh Hereedi
Ekhmim
Said or
Girgeh
el-Kirbeh
Samhoud
Farshut
Haou
Kasr e' Syad
Kenneh
Dendera
Ballas
Kott
Negadeh
Koos
THEBES
Karnak
Luxor
Erment
Ancient route from Coptos
el-Kharjeh
Great Oasis
Upper Egypt
e' Dair
Esneh
el-Kab
Edfou
Redesieh
Jebel Silsileh
Koom Ombo
Elephantine
1st Cataracts
Asouan
Philæ
EGYPT
English Miles
10 0 10 20 40 60 80
Nile
el-Kalabsheh

The Nile

Egypt, as Herodotus tells us, is the gift of the Nile, and the Nile once dominated the country even more than it does today, as these first writers show. The rising of the Nile was as significant as the changing of the seasons in other parts of the world—in fact, it created its own seasons for Egypt, as its waters provided for both the land and its people.

The Boundaries of the Country, c. 960

Ebn Haukal

When the weather becomes very warm, the water increases; and when it sinks, they sow their grain; after that, there is no necessity for water. In the land of Egypt there falls not either rain nor snow; nor in the whole country is there any running stream besides the river Nile.

The Delights of Nile Water, 1826

John Carne

Fatigued with heat and thirst we came to a few cottages in a palm-wood, and stopped to drink of a fountain of delicious water. In this northern climate no idea can be formed of the exquisite luxury of drinking in Egypt: little appetite for food is felt, but when, after crossing the burning sands, you reach the rich line of woods on the brink of the Nile, and pluck the fresh limes, and, mixing their juice with Egyptian sugar and the soft river-water, drink repeated bowls of lemonade, you feel that every other pleasure of the sense must yield to this. One then perceives the beauty and force of those similes in

Scriptures, where the sweetest emotions of the heart are compared to the assuaging of thirst in a sultry land.

Nile Water, 1825

R.R. Madden

In its wholesome properties I believe the water of the Nile exceeds that of any other river in the world. Even when turbid, as at its rise, and depositing a sediment in a tumbler, in thickness of an eighth of an inch at least, and alive with animal-culae, visible to the naked eye, even then it loses none of its salubrious qualities, but, on the contrary, by its gentle action as an aperient, it benefits health.

Notes along the Nile, 1910

Pierre Loti

A monotonous chant on three notes, which must date from the first Pharaohs, may still be heard in our days on the banks of the Nile, from the Delta as far as Nubia. At different places along the river, half-nude men, with torsos of bronze and voices all alike, intone it in the morning when they commence their endless labours and continue it throughout the day, until the evening brings repose.

Whoever has journeyed in a dahabiya up the old river will remember this song of the water-drawers, with its accompaniment, in slow cadence, of creakings of wet wood. It is the song of the 'shadûf', and the 'shadûf' is a primitive rigging which has remained unchanged since times beyond all reckoning. It is composed of a long antenna, . . . which is supported in a seesaw fashion, on an upright beam, and carries at its extremity a wooden bucket. A man, with movements of singular beauty, works it while he sings, lowers the antenna, draws the water from the river, and raises the filled bucket, which another man catches in its ascent and empties into a basin made out of the mud of the river bank. When the river is low there are three such basins, placed one above the other, as if they were stages by which the precious water mounts to the fields of corn and lucerne. And then three shadûfs, one above the other, creak together, lowering and raising their great scarabaeus' horns to the rhythm of the same song.

All along the banks of the Nile this movement of the antennae of the shadûfs is to be seen. It had its beginning in the earliest ages and is still the characteristic manifestation of human life along the river banks. It ceases only in the summer, when the river, swollen by the rains of equatorial Africa, overflows this land of Egypt, which it itself has made in the middle of the Saharan sands. But, in the winter, which is here a time of luminous drought and changeless blue skies, it is in full swing. Then every day, from dawn until the evening prayer, the men are busy at their water-drawing, transformed for the time into tireless machines, with muscles that work like metal bands. The action never changes, any more than the song, and often their thoughts must wander from their automatic toil, and lose themselves in some dream, akin to that of their ancestors who were yoked to the same rigging four or five thousand years ago. Their torsos, deluged at each rising of the overflowing bucket, stream constantly with cold water; and sometimes the wind is icy, even while the sun burns; but these perpetual workers are, as we have said, of bronze, and their bodies take no harm.

Arrangements for Traveling

Travelers in Egypt in the past had to make careful preparations for their journey up the Nile. The Arab traveler Ebn Haukal made the journey sound a great adventure and a

delight; John Fuller found the journey easy, but travelers needed advice and help from others—Harriet Martineau provided special advice for ladies. Early travelers needed a firman, or letter of introduction, from an important person in order to travel along the river.

Up Nile, c. 960
Ebn Haukal

There is not any person who knows the foundations or source of the river Nile; on this account, because it issues from a cavern in the territories of *Zingbar*, from a certain spot, which man may very nearly approach, yet never can arrive at: after this, it runs through the inhabited and desert parts of the Nubians to Misr (Egypt); and there where it first becomes a river, it is equal to the *Deljeh* and *Frat* (Tigris and Euphrates). And the water of the river Nile is the most pure and delicious of all waters on the face of the earth.

Just an Excursion, 1819

John Fuller

The narrative of a voyage on the Nile cannot be very entertaining, the incidents being little more than a repetition of rowing and towing, far and contrary winds, now and then running on a sandbank, and occasionally a mutiny of the boatmen. The police of the country was at this time good, and such perfect tranquillity prevailed that there were no 'hair-breadth 'capes', no attacks from thieves or banditti to be recorded, as in the times of the older travellers. The voyage from Cairo to the Cataract might be performed with as much security, and almost with as much ease, as an excursion on the Thames; and in my progress up and down the Nile, I fell in with not less than five or six parties of Englishmen, and several other Europeans.

The Dahabiya, 1873

Amelia Edwards

A dahabeeyah, at the first glance, is more like a civic or an Oxford University barge than anything in the shape of a boat with which we in England are familiar. It is shallow and flat-bottomed, and is adapted for either sail or rowing. It carries two masts: a big one near the prow, and a smaller one at the stern. The cabins are on deck, and occupy the after-part of the vessel; and the roof of the cabins forms the raised deck, or open-air drawing-room. This upper deck is reached from the lower deck by two little flights of steps, and is the exclusive territory of the passengers. The lower deck is the territory of the crew. A dahabeeyah is, in fact, not very unlike the Noah's Ark of our childhood, with this difference—the habitable part, instead of occupying the middle-part of the vessel, is all at one end, top-heavy and many-windowed; while the fore-deck is not more than six feet above the level of the water. The hold, however, is under the lower deck, and so counterbalances the weight at the other end. Not to multiply comparisons unnecessarily, I may say that a large dahabeeyah reminds one of old pictures of the Bucentaur, especially when the men are at their oars.

The kitchen—which is a mere shed like a Dutch oven in shape, and contains only a charcoal stove and a row of stewpans—stands between the big mast and the prow, removed as far as possible from the passengers' cabins. In this position the cook is protected from a favourable wind by his shed; but in the case of a contrary wind he is screened by an awning. How, under even the most favourable circumstances, these men can serve up the elaborate dinners which are the pride of a Nile cook's heart, is sufficiently wonderful; but how they achieve the same results when wind-storms and sand-storms are blowing, and every breath is laden with the fine grit of the desert, is little short of miraculous.

Thus far, all dahabeeyahs are alike. The cabin arrangements differ however, according to the size of the boat; and it must be remembered that in describing the Philæ, I describe a dahabeeyah of the largest build—her total length from stem to stern being just one hundred feet, and the width of her upper deck at the broadest part being little short of twenty.

Our floor being on a somewhat lower level than the men's deck, we went down three steps to the entrance door, on each side of which there was an external cupboard, one serving as a storeroom and the other as a pantry. This door led into a passage out of which opened four sleeping-cabins, two on each side. These cabins measured about eight feet in length by four and a half in width, and contained a bed, a chair, a fixed washing-stand, a looking-glass against the wall, a shelf, a row of hooks, and under each bed two large drawers for clothes.

At the end of this little passage another door opened into the dining saloon—a spacious, cheerful room, some twenty-three or twenty-four feet long, situate in the widest part of the boat, and lighted by four windows on each side and a skylight. The panelled wall and ceiling were painted in white picked out with gold; a cushioned divan covered with a smart woollen rep ran along one side; and a gay Brussels carpet adorned the floor. The dining-table stood in the centre of the room; and there was ample space for a piano, two little book-cases, and several chairs. The window-curtains and the portières were of the same rep as the divan, the prevailing colours being scarlet and orange. Add a couple of mirrors in gilt frames; a vase of flowers on the table (for we were rarely without flowers of some sort even in Nubia, where our daily bouquet had to be made with a few bean blossoms and castor-oil berries); plenty of books; the gentlemen's guns and sticks in one corner; and the hats of all the party hanging in the spaces between the windows; and it will be easy to realise the homely, habitable look of our general sitting-room. Another door and passage, opening from the upper end of the saloon, led to three more sleeping rooms, two of which were single and one double; a bath-room; a tiny back staircase leading to the upper deck; and the stern cabin saloon. This last, following the form of the stern, was semicircular, lighted by eight windows, and surrounded by a divan. Under this, as under the saloon divans, there ran a row of deep drawers, which, being fairly divided, held our clothes, wine, and books. The entire length of the dahabeeyah being exactly a hundred feet, I take the cabin part to have occupied about fifty-six or fifty-seven feet—and the lower deck to have measured the remaining forty-three feet.

For the crew there was no sleeping accommodation whatever, unless they chose to creep into the hold among the luggage and packing-cases. But this they never did. They just rolled themselves up at night, heads and all, in rough brown blankets, and lay about the lower deck like dogs.

Nile-boat Prayers, 1842

Sophia Poole

A custom which is always observed by the Arab boatmen at the commencement of a voyage much pleased me. As soon as the wind had filled our large sail, the Reis [captain] exclaimed: "El-Fat-Hah." This is the title of the opening chapter of the Koran (a short and simple prayer), which the Reis and all the crew repeated together in a low tone of voice. Would to Heaven that in this respect the example of the poor Muslim might be followed by our countrymen, that our entire dependence on the protecting providence of God might be universally acknowledged, and every journey, and every voyage, be sanctified by prayer.

Esprit du Nil, 1873

Amelia Edwards

And now we are on board and have shaken hands with the captain, and are as busy as bees; for there are cabins to be put in order, flowers to arrange, and a hundred little things to be seen to before the guests arrive. It is wonderful, however, what a few books and roses, an open piano, and a sketch or two, will do. In a few minutes the comfortless hired look has vanished, and long enough before the first comers are announced, the Philæ wears an aspect as cozy and home-like as if she had been occupied for a month.

As for luncheon, it certainly surprised the givers of the entertainment quite as much as it must have surprised their guests. Being, no doubt, a pre-arranged display of professional pride on the part of dragoman and cook, it was more like an excessive Christmas dinner than a modest midday meal. We sat through it unflinchingly, however, for about an hour and three quarters, when a startling discharge of firearms sent us all running upon deck, and created a wholesome diversion in our favour. It was the French boat signalling her departure, shaking out her big sail, and going off triumphantly.

I fear that we of the Bagstones and Philæ—being mere mortals and Englishwomen—could not help feeling just a little spiteful when we found the tricolor had started first; but then it was a consolation to know that the Frenchmen were going only to Assuân. Such is the *esprit du Nil.* The people in dahabeeyahs despise Cook's tourists; those who are bound for the Second Cataract look down with lofty compassion upon those whose ambition extends only to the First; and travellers who engage their boat by the month hold their heads a trifle higher than those who contract for the trip. We, who were going as far as we liked and for as long as we liked, could afford to be magnanimous. So we forgave the Frenchmen, went down again to the saloon, and had coffee and music.

At last all is ready. The awning that has all day roofed in the upper deck is taken down; the captain stands at the head of the steps; the steersman is at the helm; the dragoman has loaded his musket. Is the Bagstones ready? We wave a handkerchief of inquiry—the signal is answered—the mooring ropes are loosened, the sailors pole the boat off from the bank—bang go the guns, six from the Philæ, and six from the Bagstones, and away we go, our huge sail filling as it takes the wind!

Happy are the Nile travellers who start thus with a fair breeze on a brilliant afternoon. The good boat cleaves her way swiftly and steadily. Water-side palaces and gardens glide by, and are left behind. The domes and minarets of Cairo drop quickly out of sight. The mosque of the citadel, and the ruined fort that looks down upon it from the mountain ridge about, diminish in the distance. The Pyramids stand up sharp and clear.

And now, as the afternoon wanes, we draw near to a dense, wide-spreading forest of stately date-palms on the western bank, knowing that beyond them, though unseen, lie the mounds of Memphis and all the wonders of Sakkârah. Then the sun goes down behind the Libyan hills; and the palms stand out black and bronzed against a golden sky; and the Pyramids, left far behind, look grey and ghostly in the distance.

Presently, when it is quite dusk and the stars are out, we moor for the night at Bedreshayn. Such was our first day on the Nile.

At Home on the Nile, 1849

Florence Nightingale

9 December: We shall have been on board a week tomorrow, and are now thoroughly settled in our house, all our gimlets up, our divans out, our Turkish slippers (mezd) provided, and everything on its own hook, as befits such close quarters. Now, if you ask me how I like the dahabieh life, I must say I am no dahabieh bird, no divan incumbent. I do long to be wandering about the desert by myself, poking my nose into all the villages and running hither and thither, and making acquaintances *où bon me semble*. I long to be riding on my ass across the plain, I rejoice when the wind is foul, and I can get ashore. They call me 'the wild ass of the wilderness, snuffing up the wind,' because I am so fond of getting away. I dearly love our dahabieh as my home, but if it is to stay in it the whole day, as we are fain to do when the wind

is fair, that is not my way at all. However, I must tell you what walks I have had. This morning I went ashore with one of the crew at sunrise: it was cold, as cold as an English morning in October, and there was even a touch of hoar frost. But when I got under the shelter of the palm trees it was warmer. We went inland to a village, the situation of which was marked to us by its fringe of palms. Whenever you see these, you are sure of finding houses. We met a woman leading out her flock to water at a pool left by the inundation of the Nile, her black goats and white sheep. A little further on, we came to a brick-field, mud bricks laid out to bake in the sun, and full of chopped straw to make them adhere. It made one think of Rebekah and the Hebrews' task, at every turn. Then we walked round the village. But no European can have the least idea of the misery of an African village; if he has not seen it, no description brings it home. I saw a door about three feet high, of a mud hut, and peeping in, saw in the darkness nothing but a white-horned sheep, and a white hen. But something else was moving, and presently crawled out four human beings, three women and a child; they made a miserable pretence of veiling their faces before my efreet. The only reason why they had not their camel with them was because he could not get in; next door was a maize enclosure, which differed from the first only by being cleaner, and having no roof. I looked over, and saw him. . . .

All the houses in the village were exactly like this, the mud walls very thick, nearly three feet. There appeared to me to be only one den inside, but I did not go in because I had promised not. Some little things were setting out to fetch water from the Nile, each with his amphora on the head, each with a rag which scarcely descended over the body, but shrouded the head (the Arab always covers his head). . . .

The village, which seemed a considerable place, with a governor and a governor's house, possessed a khan. I peeped in. Strings of camels lay round the walls—a few inner cells behind them, roofless and floorless, showed tokens of travellers. But I was afraid of a commotion: so I veiled my face and passed on. A tray covered with the Turkish thimblefuls of coffee (which we also drink) was coming out—the only refinement the Arab possesses. In every village you see a coffee-house; generally a roofless cabin built of maize stalks, with mud benches around the inside, but always the thimblefuls of coffee, made, not like ours, but pounded, boiled for a moment, and poured off directly and drunk black. You cannot drink our coffee in this climate with impunity; it is too heating. We walked round the village, the huts all tumbled together up and down, as animals build their nests, without regularity or plan. The pigeons seemed better lodged: they had round mud cones provided for them, taller than the houses, stuck full of pots at the top for them to build in, and sticks for them to perch on. There was not much curiosity about me, though they (the Arabs, not the pigeons) could never have seen a European woman before; but they looked on with the same interest which the dogs did,—no more. By the time I came back and overtook the dahabieh, which had been tracked meanwhile for some distance (there was little wind, and that was south), the sun was high, but it was still too cold to breakfast on deck, as we have done once.

Onboard a River Steamer, 1863

Lucie Duff Gordon

After infinite delays and worries, we are at last on board, and shall sail tomorrow morning. After all was comfortably settled, Ismail Pasha sent for all the steamers up to Rhoda, near Minieh, and at the same time ordered a Turkish General to come up instantly somehow. So Latif Pasha, the head of the steamers, had to turn me out of the best cabin, and if I had not come myself, and taken rather forcible possession of the forecastle cabin, the servants of the Turkish General would not have allowed Omar to embark the baggage. He had been waiting all the morning in despair on the bank; but at four I arrived, and ordered the *hammals* to carry the goods into the fore-cabin, and walked on board myself, where the Arab captain pantomimically placed me in the right eye and on the top of his head.

Once installed, this became a harem, and I may defy the Turkish Effendi with success. I have got a good-sized cabin with good, clean divans round three sides for Sally [Duff Gordon's English maid] and myself.

Omar will sleep on deck and cook where he can. A poor Turkish lady is to inhabit a sort of dusthole by the side of my cabin; if she seems decent, I will entertain her hospitably. There is no furniture of any sort but the divan, and we cook our own food, bring our own candles, jugs, basins, beds and everything. If Sally and I were not such complete Arabs we should think it very miserable; but as things stand this year we say, *Alhamdulillah*—it is no worse!

Luckily it is a very warm night, so we can make our arrangements unchilled. There is no door to the cabin, so we nail up an old plaid, and, as no one ever looks into a harem, it is quite enough. All on board are Arabs—captain, engineer and men. An English Sitt [lady] is a novelty, and the captain is unhappy that things are not *alla Franca* for me. We are to tow three dahabiehs—M. Mounier's, one belonging to the envoy from the Sultan of Darfur, and another. Three steamers were to have done it, but the Pasha had a fancy for all the boats, and so our poor little craft must do her best. Only fancy the Queen ordering all the river steamers up to Windsor!

At Minieh the Turkish General leaves us, and we shall have the boat to ourselves, so the captain has just been down to tell me. I should like to go with the gentlemen from Darfur, as you may suppose. See what strange combinations of people float on old Nile. Two English women, one French (Mme Mounier), one Frenchman, Turks, Arabs, Negroes, Circassians, and men from Darfur, all in one party; perhaps the third boat contains some other strange element. The Turks are from Constantinople and can't speak Arabic, and make faces at the muddy river water, which, indeed, I would rather have filtered. . . .

I am quite surprised to see how well these men manage their work. The boat is quite as clean as an English boat as crowded could be kept, and the engine in beautiful order. The head-engineer, Achmet Effendi, and indeed all the crew and captain too, wear English clothes and use the universal, 'All right, stop her—fooreh (full) speed, half speed—turn her head,' etc. I was delighted to hear, 'All right—go ahead—*el-Fathah*' in one breath. Here we always say the *Fathah* (first chapter of the Koran, nearly identical with the Lord's Prayer) when starting on a journey, concluding a bargain, etc. The combination was very quaint.

On the Boats, 1990

Deborah Manley

Today, unless you are adventurous enough to sail down the Nile by felucca, your journey will be in one of the 200 or so river boats that act like floating hotels between Luxor and Aswan. Hemmed in by the barrages and the 'British' dam at Aswan, they move up and down between the two all year long. They glory in great classical names like *Rameses*, *King of the River*, or *Nefertiti*, *King Tut*, *Ra* even, or have names which compete for today's dreams like *Moon River* or *Nile Splendor* (note the US spelling). Our boat was the MV *Atlas*, one of the smaller, less grandiloquent crafts, but comfy, well run and of a pleasing size. Sadly for the company which owned it (these floating hotels are owned by tourist companies or by the hotel chains who own the land-based hotels too), but pleasantly for us, it was hardly more than half full. When at capacity the *Atlas* would hold eighty-five passengers and a crew of sixty. These crew members would encompass a manager and two assistant managers (the manager is effectively the captain and chief executive, purser and PR manager rolled into one); a pilot and two assistants, an engineer and five assistants, a *maitre d'* and ten stewards, a housekeeper with ten staff, three barmen and nine sailors who doubled as porters, and ten service staff. In addition each tourist language group is accompanied by its own tour guide.

At any one time about a fifth of this hierarchy will be on ten days' leave after six weeks on the river. Many of them are able to visit their homes when the boats dock at Luxor or Aswan, but others come from as far away as Cairo.

How do all these people come to their jobs on the boats? For all except the manual workers there are various forms of apprenticeships. Some will have gone to hotel-management school; the guides will have done a university tourist course; the stewards come from long lines of Nubian domestic staff with experience passed down through the families. The pilots learn the river on feluccas and graduate up through work boats to the helm of a floating hotel, learning as they go. There is a lot of camaraderie among the pilots, who wave and shout across to one another from boat to boat as they pass—and give blasts of their horns.

We joined the helmsman one morning as he zigzagged along past a village at the bend of the river. Despite his pointing them out to us, we could barely discern the slight ripple that warned of a sandbank below the surface and guided the assured skill of his actions. Nowadays, since the High Dam, the river at least stays in one place. No longer do unexpected shoals catch unwary boats as they frequently did in the past.

At Aswan each company has its own anchorage. The Nile side is lined by arches on which are listed each company's boats, with steps dropping down the steep bank to the mooring. In Luxor and along the river it is a free for all, but the *Atlas* appears to have clout and seniority and often moors beside Luxor temple.

The boats may be lined up two or more deep. We briefly were boat eight on the outer edge. All the boats have a wide central reception area, and to reach an outside boat you walk straight through all of them from the shore.

Only on the River, 1836

John Lloyd Stephens

I have heard all manner of opinion expressed in regard to a voyage on the Nile; and may be allowed, perhaps, to give my own. Mrs. S. used frequently to say that, although she had traveled in France, Switzerland, Germany, Italy, and Sicily, she had never enjoyed a journey so much before, and was always afraid that it would end too soon. Another lady's sentiments, expressed in my hearing, were just the contrary. For myself, being alone, and not in very good health, I had some heavy moments; but I have no hesitation in saying that, with a friend, a good boat well fitted up, books, guns, plenty of time, and a cook like Michel, a voyage on the Nile would exceed any traveling within experience. The perfect freedom from all restraint, and from the conventional trammels of civilized society, form an episode in a man's life that is vastly agreeable and exciting. Think of not shaving for two months, of washing your shirts in the Nile, and wearing them without being ironed. True, these things are not absolutely necessary; but who would go to Egypt to travel as he does in Europe? "Away with all fantasies and fetters" is the motto of the tourist. We throw aside pretty much everything except our pantaloons; and a generous rivalry in long beards and soiled linen is kept up with exceeding spirit. You may go ashore whenever you like, and stroll through the little villages, and be stared at by the Arabs, or walk along the banks of the river till darkness covers the earth; shooting pigeons, and sometimes pheasants and hares, besides the odd shots from the deck of your boat at geese, crocodiles, and pelicans. And then it is so ridiculously cheap an amusement. You get your boat with ten men for thirty or forty dollars a month, fowls for three piasters (about a shilling) a pair, a sheep for half or three-quarters of a dollar and eggs almost for the asking. You sail under your own country's banner; and, when you walk along the river, if the Arabs look particularly black and truculent, you proudly feel that there is safety in its folds. From time to time you hear that a French or English flag has passed so many days before you, and you meet your fellow-voyagers with a freedom and cordiality which exist nowhere but on the Nile.

Weather Conditions

Travel along the Nile often proved to be a challenge, as the weather could change swiftly. While Amelia Edwards found herself becalmed on the river, Florence Nightingale discovered that a khamsin wind blowing from the south could wreak deathly destruction.

Tracking, 1873

Amelia Edwards

The good wind continued to blow all that night; but fell at sunrise, precisely when we were about to start. The river now stretched away before us, smooth as glass, and there was nothing for it, said Reïs Hassan, but tracking. We had heard of tracking often enough since coming to Egypt, but without having any definite idea of the process. Coming on deck, however, before breakfast, we found nine of our poor fellows harnessed to a rope like barge-horses, towing the huge boat against the current. Seven of the M.B.'s crew similarly harnessed, followed at a few yard's distance. The two ropes met and crossed and dipped into the water together. Already our last night's mooring-place was out of sight, and the Pyramid of Ouenephes [the Step Pyramid of Saqqara] stood up amid its lesser brethren on the edge of the desert, as if bidding us good-bye. But the sight of the trackers jarred, somehow, with the placid beauty of the picture. We got used to it, as one gets used to everything in time; but it looked like slaves' work, and shocked our English notions disagreeably.

Thus the morning passes. We sit on deck writing letters; reading; watching the sunny river-side pictures that glide by at foot's pace and are so long in sight. Palmgroves, sandbanks, patches of fuzzy-headed dura and fields of some yellow-flowering herb, succeed each other. A boy plods along the bank, leading a camel. They go slowly; but they soon leave us behind. A native boat meets us, floating down side-wise with the current. A girl comes to the water's edge with a great empty jar on her head, and waits to fill it till the trackers have gone by. The pigeon-towers of a mud-village peep above a clump of lebbek trees, a quarter of a mile inland. Here a solitary brown man, with only a felt skull-cap on his head and a slip of a scanty tunic fastened about his loins, works a shâdûf, stooping and rising, stooping and rising, with the regularity of a pendulum. It is the same machine which we shall see by and by depicted in the tombs at Thebes; and the man is so evidently an ancient Egyptian, that we find ourselves wondering how he escaped being mummified four or five thousand years ago.

By and by, a little breeze springs up. The men drop the rope and jump on board—the big sail is set—the breeze freshens—and, away we go again, as merrily as the day we left Cairo.

The Khamsin, 1849
Florence Nightingale

About three, the khamsin increased; it was a wind like this which destroyed six years ago a caravan of 300 camels belonging to Mehemet Ali. The air became filled with sand. The river seemed turned upside down, and flowing bottom upwards, the whirlwind of sand from the desert literally covering it. We could not see across the river; and when we could stand upon deck, which was not often, our eyes were completely filled and our faces covered with sand. As to the Critic making Thames *not* to walk between his banks, he does not deserve the credit of originality for that idea, for Nile invented the plan first, and today instead of walking between his banks, his banks walked between him. I saw the sand blown up into a ridge *upon* the water, and it looked as if you could have passed the river on dry ground, only the dry ground was on the top. I am glad to have seen it, for I should never have believed in it if I had not, and I give you leave not to believe. By this time Nile seemed to be walking with his bed on his head; but it was no beneficent miracle, like the paralytic man's, for it looked as if earth, air, and water had been blasted together into one whirlwind of sand. We could not wash, for it was no use fishing for water in the Nile; instead of water he gave us a stone, i.e. a sand-bank. The waves were as high as when there is a moderate sea in the [English] Channel, and the wind was hot. It grew dark, and the blast increased so, that we drove a stake into the bank and fastened a rope to it for the night.

Presently Paolo rushed in for one of the guns, which was always kept loaded. He said he saw a strange boat coming in sight. I ran out on deck after him and sure enough, in pitchy darkness, I saw one of the dahabiehs which had overtaken us in the afternoon, floating past us, bottom upwards; nothing to be seen of her passengers. She struck in the sand just astern of us, and remained fast there. By this time the wind had increased so much, and we bumped so incessantly that we were afraid the rope would not hold, and we put out another. I could not help laughing, in the middle of all this, at the figure of our Reis, who had squatted himself at the bottom of our little boat (which was between the dahabieh and the bank), and sat there smoking his pipe, and taking no further interest in the question. If the rope wouldn't hold it wouldn't, and why should he be disturbed?

I did not go to bed—we bumped incessantly, and at the stern especially so hard that we thought we must spring a leak. It was so dark that we could see nothing, but in the morning we found that our boat had been astride of the poor wreck all night, which had been whirled round by the eddy under us. At dawn I looked out: she had entirely gone to pieces. Nothing was left of her but a few of the cabin planks, which our boat picked up, a chest of clothes which we saved, and her oranges floating in the whirlpool. I never saw anything so affecting as those poor oranges—the last luxury of their life in the midst of death.

Torrents of rain were falling—our cabin roof was completely soaked through—the sky was still one heavy mass, but the wind had a little fallen, and we struggled on, towed by the wretched crew, their teeth chattering, dripping with wet, and evidently thinking the Day of Judgement, the end of the world, was come (for to them rain is much what to us English an earthquake might be) to Manfaloot, which we reached about twelve. There we learnt the fate of the five boats which passed us yesterday to windward: four had gone down, and of their passengers, twenty (including women and children) had been lost.

Wind-bound, 1836

John Lloyd Stephens

On the eighth I had not made much more than fifty miles, and the wind was still ahead, and blowing stronger than ever; indeed, it seemed as if this morning, for the first time, it had really commenced in earnest. I became desperate and went ashore, resolved to wear it out. We were lying along the bank, on the Libyan side, in company with fifteen or twenty boats wind-bound like ourselves. It was near a little mud village, of which I forget the name, and several Bedouin tents were on the bank, in one of which I was sitting smoking a pipe. The wind was blowing down with a fury I have never seen surpassed in a gale at sea, bringing with it the light sand of the desert, and at times covering the river with a thick cloud which prevented my seeing across it. A clearing up for a moment showed a boat of the largest class, heavily laden, and coming down with astonishing velocity; it was like the flight of an enormous bird. She was under bare poles, but small portions of the sail had got loose, and the Arabs were out on the very ends of the long spars getting them in. One of the boatmen, with a rope under his arm, had plunged into the river, and with strong swimming reached the bank, where a hundred men ran to his assistance. Their united strength turned her bows around, upstream, but nothing could stop her; stern foremost, she dragged the whole posse of Arabs to the bank, and broke away from them perfectly ungovernable; whirling around, her bows pitched into our fleet with a loud crash; and tore away several of the boats, and carrying one off, fast locked as in a death-grasp, she resumed her headlong course down the river. They had gone but a few rods when the stranger pitched her bows under and went down in a moment, bearing her helpless companion also to the bottom.

Nile Creatures

The creatures of the Nile accompanied travelers on their journeys, sometimes intimately, as George Melly discovered. Crocodiles, no longer found below the Aswan High Dam,

were often the cause of great excitement for the early traveler, as were locusts when they swarmed in their millions, destroying crops and turning the sky black.

Melancholy and Invaders, 1851

George Melly

The huge sails were loosed, and expanded to a mild evening breeze, with just strength enough to blow out the folds of our Union Jack, which flew proudly over us. It was an exciting moment, but I cannot say that it was wholly free from melancholy; for while we looked up the mighty river with eager impatience for the wonders it was to disclose, we could not but feel that, when anchor was hauled up, we threw off our last hold of society, completely severed ourselves from all communication with our friends, and crossed the confines of barbarism. But this impression was not allowed to deepen, and speedily gave way before our earnest longing for new objects and other regions.

It was late before I went to bed, and I had scarcely fallen asleep when I was aroused by a pressure on my feet. At first, I thought someone must be sitting upon me, and was about to remonstrate, but a sudden squeaking undeceived me, and I discovered that the intruders were three enormous rats, who had stretched themselves very comfortably on the coverlet. Fortunately my boots were at hand, and I flung one into the midst of them, on which they scampered off in great dismay, vehemently protesting against such uncourteous treatment. I then got up, and barricaded the door, which I was assisted in doing by one of our servants.

Timseach! Timseach! 1843

Eliot Warburton

The first time that a man fires at a crocodile is an epoch in his life. We had only now arrived in the waters where they abound, for it is a curious fact that none are ever seen below Mineyeh, though Herodotus speaks of them as fighting with the dolphins at the mouths of the Nile. A prize had been offered for the first man who detected a crocodile, and the crew had now been for two days on the alert in search of them. Buoyed up with the expectation of such game, we had latterly reserved our fire for them exclusively, and the wild duck and turtle[doves], nay, even the vulture and the eagle had swept past, or soared above us in security.

At length the cry of "Timseach! Timseach!" was heard from half a dozen claimants of the proffered prize, and half a dozen black fingers were eagerly pointed to a spit of sand, on which were strewn apparently some logs of trees. It was a Covey of Crocodiles! Hastily and silently the boat was run on shore. R. was ill, so I had the enterprise to myself, and clambered up the steep bank with a quicker pulse than when I first levelled a rifle at a Highland deer. My intended victims might have prided themselves on their superior nonchalance; and, indeed, as I approached them, there seemed to be a sneer on their ghastly mouths and winking eyes. Slowly they rose, one after the other, and waddled to the water, all but one, the most gallant or most gorged of the party. He lay still until I was within a hundred yards of them; then, slowly rising up on his fin-like legs, he lumbered towards the river, looking askance at me with an expression of countenance that seemed to say: "He can do me no harm; however, I may as well have a swim." I took aim at the throat of the supercilious brute, and, as soon as my hand steadied, the very pulsation of my finger pulled the trigger. Bang! went the gun; whiz! flew the bullet; and my excited ear could catch the *thud* with which it plunged into the scaly leather of his neck. His waddle became a plunge, the waves closed over him, and the sun shone on the calm water, as I reached the brink of the shore, that was still indented by the waving of his gigantic tail. But there is blood upon the water, and he rises for a moment to the surface.

"A hundred piastres for the timseach," I exclaimed, and half a dozen Arabs plunged into the stream.

There he rises again, and the men dash at him as if he hadn't a tooth in his head. Now he is gone, the waters close over him, I never saw him since.

Crocodiles and Sekenkour, c. 960
Ebn Haukal

The Nile produces crocodiles, and the fish *sekenkour*; and there is also a species of fish, called *raadah*, which if any person take it in hand while it is alive, that person will be affected by a trembling of his body; when dead, this fish resembles other fish. The crocodile's head is very long, so long as to be one half of his whole form, and he has such teeth, that, if a lion were to come within their hold, he would be destroyed. It sometimes happens that the crocodile comes out of the water on dry ground; but he has not then the same powers as when in the water. His skin is so hard that it resists the blows of all weapons when stricken on the back; they then wound him where the forelegs join the body, and between the thighs. The *sekenkour* [skink] is a species of the crocodile, but the crocodile has *hands and feet*; and they use the *sekenkour* in medical and culinary preparations. This creature is not found anywhere but in the River Nile.

Locusts, 1827

Robert Hay

This morning the cries of the people were heard on both sides of the river lamenting the certain loss of their crops and calling on God and the Prophet to spare them. Last night's (southerly) wind had brought down a large flight of locusts which now darkened the air and was settling on every green spot they could find. The whole morning they were very numerous but not as they were at first, as a great proportion of them had settled.

About one o'clock I went out of the boat and my surprise was indescribable when I witnessed the scene of devastation that lay before me. A field of young dura was eaten level with the ground, so that there existed scarcely part of a stalk! Yet notwithstanding the clearance they made, the ground was literally yellow with them, and I think without any exaggeration, and even perhaps I am within bounds when I say they were 40 to each square foot! How frightful then must have been their numbers when we consider the distance they spread themselves? As we walked through [a field] they rose like a swarm of bees, at this time the air was so filled with them that it had perfectly the appearance of a heavy fall of snow which appearance was increased by the thickness of the atmosphere. . . .

The water wheels had ceased to work and everything wore so sad an aspect that we could not feel too thankful that our own country is not visited by such a dreadful and appalling scourge! Labour lost, and money that can be ill afforded spent. All to begin again! and perhaps it may be again the fate of the second crop to be devoured in a few hours after weeks of labour!!!

Along the banks every tree and bush was yellow with the crop of locusts that it bore; all verdure was fast disappearing and in a great many instances, perfectly gone. Sunt trees and doums. Palm-trees with their fruit. The cotton plant. The dura and even the coarse grass all shared the same fate!

I believe it almost impossible for anyone to conceive such a scene without having witnessed it. For though they may give credit to what has been related by so many, they cannot form an idea of the scene of rapid desolation that follows the appearance of this destructive insect.

Creatures Come Down to Drink, 1817

Charles Irby and James Mangles

Wednesday, July 23. It was curious to observe in the morning, on the smooth surface of the sand, drifted by the night breeze, the tracks of the snakes, lizards, animals, etc., etc. which had come down to the water's side during the night to drink; and we could plainly discern the traces of their return to their solitary haunts in the desert. Sometimes their track indicated the presence of reptiles of considerable size; and with these proofs of their nocturnal movements, we easily accounted for the dread our guides expressed of walking near the water's side the night we returned from the second cataract.

Up to Luxor

After the watery tenderness of the Delta and the strident grandeur of Cairo and the almost overwhelming magnificence of the Pyramids and Sphinx, travelers up the Nile met new experiences as they were transported toward Upper

Egypt. The fascination of life along the Nile was reflected in the wall-paintings at Beni Hassan, and all around the travelers saw what Ibn Jubayr described in 1183 as "wondrous things."

The Constant Change of Scene, 1833
Robert Curzon

Nothing can be more secure and peaceable than a journey on the Nile, as everyone knows nowadays. Floating along in a boat like a house, which stops and goes on whenever you like, you have no cares or troubles but those which you bring with you. . . . I can imagine nothing more delightful than a voyage up the Nile with agreeable companions in the winter, when the climate is perfection. There are the most wonderful antiquities for those who interest themselves in the remains of bygone days; famous shooting on the banks of the river; capital dinners, if you know how to make proper arrangements, comfortable quarters, and a constant change of scene.

Nile by Night and Dawn, 1843

Eliot Warburton

This sailing on the moon-lit Nile has an inexpressible charm; every sight is softened, every sound is musical, every air breathes balm. The pyramids, silvered by the moon, tower over the dark palms, and the broken ridges of the Arabian hills stand clearly out from the star-spangled sky. Distant lights, gleaming faintly among the scarce seen minarets, mark the site of Cairo, whose voices come at intervals as faintly to the ear. Sometimes the scream of a startled pelican, or the gurgle of some huge fish as he wallows in the water, may disturb the silence for a moment, but the calm that follows is only the more profound.

All nature seems so tranced, and all the world wound in such a dream, that we can scarcely realise our own identity: hark to the jackal's cry among the Moslem tombs! See where the swarthy pilot sits, statue-like with his turban and flowing beard; those plains before us have been trod by Pharaohs; these waters have borne Cleopatra; yonder citadel was the home of Saladin! We need not sleep to dream.

The night is gone—gone like a passing shadow; the sun springs suddenly into the throne of purple and rose-coloured clouds that the mist has left for him. There is scarcely a dawn: even now it was night—then day—suddenly as a cannon's flash.

Our boat lay moored to the bank. Mahmoud started to his feet, and shouted "Yallough!" like a trumpet. Till then the deck seemed vacant; the crew sleeping in grave-like apertures between the planks, wrapped in their white capotes—a shroud-like garment that gives to their resurrection a rather ghastly appearance. All nature seems to waken now; flocks of turtle-doves are rustling round the villages; dogs are barking the flocks to pasture; cocks are crowing; donkeys are braying; water-wheels are creaking; and the Moslems prostrate themselves in prayer, with forehead to the ground, or hands crossed upon their bosoms, their eyes motionless, and their lips quivering with the first chapter of the Koran.

For my own part, a plunge into the Nile constitutes the principal part of the toilette in which razor or looking-glass are unknown. Re-dressed, re-turbaned, and re-seated on my carpet, Abdallah, with a graceful obeisance, presents a chibouque of fragrant latakeea, as different from our coarse English tobacco as a pastille is from burnt feathers; and Mahmoud offers a little cup of coffee's very essence. In the mean time the crew are pitching the tent upon a little lawn beneath some palm-trees, for yonder forest shadows the ruins of Memphis, and the gardens wherein Moses used to wander with Pharaoh's daughter.

So Much to See, 1848

Harriet Martineau

And when on board, there was so much to be seen on the ordinary banks that I was rarely in the cabin. Before breakfast, I was walking on deck. After breakfast, I was sewing, reading, or writing, or idling on deck, under the shade of the awning. After dinner, we all came out eagerly, to enjoy the last hour of sunshine, and the glories of the sunset and the after-glow, and the rising of the moon and constellations. And sorry was I every night when it was ten o'clock, and I must go under a lower roof than that of the dazzling heavens. All these hours of our first days had their ample amusement from what we saw on the banks alone, till we could penetrate further. . . .

There was the pretty sight of the preparation of the drying banks for the new crop;—the hoeing with the short, heavy antique hoe. And the harrow, drawn by a camel, would appear on the ridge of the bank. . . . Then, there were the endless manoeuvres of innumerable birds, about the islets and rocks: and buffalo, here and there, swimming from bank to bank, and finding it, at last, no easy matter to gain the land.—Then, there was the ferryboat, with its ragged sail, and its motley freight of turbaned men, veiled women, naked children, brown sheep, frightened asses, and imperturbable buffalo.—Then, there were the long palisades of sugar canes edging the banks; or the steep slopes, all soft and bright with the springing wheat or the bristling lupins. Then, there were the villages, with their somewhat pyramidal houses, their clouds of pigeons, and their shelter of palms: or, here and there, a town, with its minarets rising out of its cincture of acacia.

And it was not long before we found our sight sharpened to discern holes in the rocks, far or near,—holes so squared at the entrance as to hint of sculpture or painting within.—And, then, as the evening drew on, there was the sinking of the sun, and the coming out of the colours which had been discharged by the glare in the middle of the day. The vast and dreary and hazy Arabian desert became yellow, melting into the purple hills; the muddy waters took a lilac hue; and the shadows of the sharp-cut banks were as blue as the central sky. As for the moon, we could, for the first time in our lives, see her the first night;—the slenderest thread of cup-like form, visible for a few minutes after sunset; the old moon being so clearly marked as to be seen by itself after the radiant rim was gone. I have seen it behind a palm, or resting on the ridge of a mountain like a copper ball. And when the fuller moon came up from the east, and I, forgetting the clearness of the sky, have been struck by the sudden dimness, and have looked up to watch her passing behind a cloud, it was delicious to see, instead of any cloud, the fronds of the palm waving upon her disk.

Life in the Grottoes, 1860

Mrs. M. Carey

We reached the Grottoes at last. They are cut along the side of the hill, at a distance of about two miles from the village. Those to the south pleased us extremely. They are of the oldest style of Egyptian architecture, and very elegant. The columns represent four stems of water plants, supporting a capital in the form of lotus or papyrus buds. The transverse section of these grottoes is very elegant, and the architecture resembles a depressed pediment, extending over the columns, and resting at either end on a low pilaster. The simplicity and elegance of the style and device strike the eye at once. The walls of all the grottoes are covered with various interesting coloured devices.

When the eye has become accustomed to the partial light within, these can be gradually made out, and we took great delight in tracing the following subjects:— the tillage of the ground; making of ropes; weaving of linen cloth; the manufacture of jewellery and pottery; various hunting scenes; men tending sick cattle; feeding the oryx; fishing-nets; clap-nets; pressing wine in a wine-press;

men wrestling; women playing at ball, and performing various feats of agility in a most unwomanlike manner; both sexes receiving the bastinado, the men laid on the ground, the women sitting; playing the harp; games of draughts and 'mora'; a barber shaving a customer; some cranes; a very curious procession of strangers, supposed, from their dress, beards and sandals, and boots, to be some Asiatic people, being presented, probably, to the owner of the tomb, and offering him presents of the produce of their country; finally, boats bearing the dead body to its place of sepulture; these, and many others, we examined with interest, by the assistance of *Murray's Handbook* and Wilkinson's *Ancient Egyptians*. The curious custom is also seen here of writing over the subject represented the name of what it was intended to represent. In one instance, in particular, it appeared very desirable; if the artist did intend in this case to represent kids feeding upon a vine, we should certainly have wished to see written up over them, "This is a vine, these are kids."

The Temple of Hermopolis at Minya, 1813
James Silk Buckingham

Returning to the boat, we continued our course on the Nile, landing at Minieh, a populous and flourishing town on the western bank, and thence onward to the ruins of Antinoe, on the eastern: a city built by the Roman Emperor Adrian, and so called after his favourite, the beautiful Antinous, who was drowned in the Nile. I passed a whole day within these ruins, which have all the grandeur of Roman times, the architecture being chiefly Corinthian; and the number of edifices, colonnades, and partially dilapidated public structures that still remain, make up a scene of great beauty, though in desolation.

On the following day I visited the first Egyptian architectural monument to be seen on ascending the Nile, namely, the portico of the Temple of Hermopolis. It was like passing from St Paul's Cathedral to Westminster Abbey; the former well calculated to excite admiration for its noble proportions and fine architectural effect, but the latter inspiring feelings of awe and devotion, amid the 'dim religious light' of its coloured glass, lofty aisles, and fretted roof.

A single paragraph from my journal of that day will express this more fully:

When I dismounted and approached its gigantic columns, I know not whether their colossal size, their rich invention, or their exquisite finish attracted my regard more strongly; but this I perfectly remember, that—while lost amidst the commingled feelings which the pillared portico of this massive pile inspired, regretting the lost language of its inscriptive figures, and admiring the happiest union of pure simplicity, luxuriant ornament, and everlasting strength—I felt, beneath its awe-inspiring roof, a sensation of humility and devotion, which Antinoe, with all its beauties of the picturesque, or all the sadness of its desolating ruins, had not the power to create.

Asyut and Explorations, 1836

John Lloyd Stephens

Asyut stands about a mile and a half from the river, in one of the richest valleys of the Nile. At the season of inundation, when the river rolls down with all its majesty, the whole intermediate country is overflowed; and boats of the largest size, steering their course over the waste of waters by the projecting tops of the palm-trees, come to anchor under the walls of the city. A high causeway from the river to the city crosses the plain, a comparatively unknown and unnoticed, but stupendous work, which for more than three thousand years has resisted the headlong current of the Nile at its highest, and now stands, like the Pyramids, not so striking, but an equally enduring, and perhaps more really wonderful monument of Egyptian labour. A short distance before reaching the city, on the right, are the handsome palace and garden of Ibrahim Pasha. A stream winds through the valley, crossed by a stone bridge, and over this is the entrance-gate of the city. The governor's palace, the most imposing and best structure I had seen since the Citadel at Cairo, standing first within the walls, seemed like a warder at the door. . . .

I do not believe that the contents of all the bazaars in Asyut, one of the largest towns in Egypt, were worth as much as the stocks of an ordinary dealer in dry goods in Broadway, New York. But these are not the things for which the traveller stops at Asyut. On the lofty mountains overlooking this richest valley of the Nile, and protecting it from the Libyan Desert, is a long range of tombs, the burial place of the ancient Egyptians; and looking for a moment at the little Mohamedan burying ground, the traveller turns with wonder from the little city he has left, and asks:

"Where is the great city which had its graves in the sides of yonder mountain? Where are the people who despised the earth as a burial-place, and made for themselves tombs in the eternal granite?"

The mountain is about as far from the city as the river, and the approach to it is by another strong causeway over the same beautiful plain. Leaving our donkeys at its foot, and following in the nimble footsteps of my little Arab girl, we climbed by a steep ascent to the first range of tombs. They were the first I had seen, and are but little visited by travellers and though afterward I saw all that were in Egypt, I still consider these well worth a visit. . . . The ceilings were covered with paintings, finished with exquisite taste and delicacy, and in some places fresh as if just executed; and on the halls were hieroglyphics enough to fill volumes. . . . The back chambers were so dark, and their atmosphere was so unwholesome, that it was unpleasant, and perhaps unsafe, to explore them; if we went in far there was always a loud rushing noise, as if their innermost recesses might now be the abode of wild beasts. Wishing to see what caused the noise, and at the same time to keep out of harm's way, we stationed ourselves near the back door of the entrance-chamber, and I fired my gun within; a stream of fire lighted up the darkness of the sepulchral chamber, and the report when grumbling and roaring into the innermost recesses, rousing their occupants to frenzy. There was the noise like the rushing of a strong wind; the light was dashed from my companion's hand; a soft skinny substance struck against my face; and thousands of bats, wild with fright, came whizzing forth from every part of the tomb to the only avenue of escape. We threw ourselves down and allowed the ugly frightened birds to pass over us, and then hurried out ourselves. For a moment I felt guilty; the beastly birds, driven to the light of day, were dazzled by the glorious sun, and, flying and whirling blindly about, were dashing themselves against the rocky side of the mountain and falling dead at its base.

Coming upon Dendera by Night, 1829
Jean-François Champollion

The moonlight was magnificent, and we were only at a distance of one hour from the temples; could we resist the temptation? I ask this of the coldest of mortals! To eat and to leave immediately was the work of a moment: alone without guides, but armed to the teeth, we set off

across the fields, presuming that the temples were in a direct line with our boat. We walked like this, singing the most recent opera marches, for an hour and a half, without finding anything. Finally a man was discovered; we called to him and he bolted, taking us for Bedouin, for, dressed in the eastern manner and covered with a great white hooded cape, we resembled to the Egyptian man a tribe of Bedouins, whilst a European might have taken us without hesitation for a guerrilla force of Carthusian monks armed with guns, sabres and pistols. The runaway was brought to me—I ordered him to lead us to the temples. This poor devil, barely reassured at first, took us along a good route and finished by walking with good grace; thin, dry, black, covered with old rags, this was a *walking mummy*, but he guided us rather well and we treated him the same way.

The temples finally appeared to us. I will not try to describe the impression which the great propylon and especially the portico of the great temple made on us. One can measure it easily, but to give an idea of it is impossible. It is grace and majesty brought together in the highest degree.

Akhmim: A Wondrous Thing, 1183
Ibn Jubayr

The most remarkable of the temples of the world talked of for their wonder is the great temple east of the city and below its walls. Its length is two hundred and twenty cubits, and its breadth one hundred and sixty. The people of these parts know it as *birba*, and thus too are known all their temples and ancient constructions. This great temple is supported by forty columns, beside its walls, the circumference of each column being fifty spans and the distance between them thirty spans. Their capitals are of great size and perfection, cut in an unwonted fashion and angulated in ornate style as if done by turners. The whole is embellished with many colours, lapis lazuli and others. The columns are carved in low relief from top to bottom. Over the capital of each column and stretching to its neighbour is a great slab of carved stone, the biggest of which we measured and found to be fifty-six spans in length, ten in width, and eight in depth.

The ceiling of this temple is wholly formed of slabs of stone so wonderfully joined as to seem to be one single piece; and over it all are disposed rare paintings and uncommon colours, so that the beholder conceives the roof to be of carved wood. Each slab has a different painting. Some are adorned with comely pictures of birds with outstretched wings making the beholder believe they are about to fly away; others are embellished with images of men, very beautiful to look upon and of elegant form, each having a distinctive shape, for example holding a statuette or a weapon, or a bird, or a chalice, or making sign to another with the hand, together with other forms it would take too long to describe and which words are not adequate to express.

Within and without this great temple, both in its upper and lower parts, are pictures all of varied form and description. Some are dreadful, inhuman forms that terrify the beholder and fill him with wonder and amazement. There was hardly the space of an awl or needle-hole which did not have an image or engraving or some hieroglyphic writing that is not understood. This remarkable decoration which can be wrought from hard stone where it cannot be worked in soft wood, covers the whole of this vast and splendid temple, in wonder at which the beholder might conceive that all time spent in its adornment, embellishment, and beautifying would be too short. Glory to the Creator of wondrous things. There is no God but He.

Luxor

Many travelers had translated Homer's words on Thebes in the schoolroom, and coming to Luxor was a high point of their travels. The magnificence of Karnak silenced Amelia Edwards; across the Nile, the isolated Valley of the Kings and its tombs awed the travelers.

Luxor—Ancient Thebes, 1846

Cuthbert Young

Thebes—old Egyptian Thebes—what strange ideas does the word conjure up! It was very different from any of my conceptions, and its real character is best told by saying that it is strangely old and strangely interesting. I had most reluctantly passed it on our upward voyage, and now it was with feelings of an intense kind that I put my foot for the first time on Theban soil.

Hundred-Gated Thebes, 1817

Charles Irby and James Mangles

We now returned to Luxor, and having seen every thing we began to think of returning. I cannot quit Thebes, however, without a few observations; most travellers, when speaking of this ancient capital, make mention of the lines of Homer, wherein he alludes to Thebes in such glowing characters. I shall give you Alexander Pope's translation of the passage, and then add a few observations which occurred to me on the spot.

Not all proud Thebes' unrivalled walls contain
The world's great Empress on th' Egyptian plain;
That spreads her conquest o'er a thousand states,
And pours her heroes through a hundred gates,
Two hundred horsemen, and two hundred cars,
From each wide portal issuing to the wars.

In our researches throughout the whole of the Theban ruins we could not meet with any remains of either walls or gates, unless the term is applied to the pylons and other buildings which constitute the approach to the sacred edifices.

Good Morning, Luxor! 1873
Amelia Edwards

Coming on deck the third morning after leaving Denderah, we found the dahabeeyah decorated with palm-branches, our sailors in their holiday turbans, and Reis Hassan *en grande tenue*; that is to say in shoes and stockings, which he only wore on very great occasions.

"Nehârak-sa'id—good morning—Luxor!" said he all in one breath.

It was a hot, hazy morning, with dim ghosts of mountains glowing through the mist, and a warm wind blowing.

We ran to the side; looked eagerly; but could see nothing. Still the Captain smiled and nodded; and the sailors ran hither and thither, sweeping and garnishing; and Egendi, to whom his worst enemy could not have imputed the charge of bashfulness, said "Luxor—kharûf [sheep]—all right!" every time he came near us. We had read and dreamed so much about Thebes, and it had always seemed so far away, that but for this delicate allusion to the promised sheep, we could hardly have believed we were really drawing nigh unto those famous shores. About ten, however, the mist was lifted away like a curtain, and we saw to the left a rich plain studded with palm-groves; to the right a broad margin of cultivated lands bounded by a bold range of limestone mountains; and on the farthest horizon another range, all grey and shadowy.

"Karnak—Gournah—Luxor!" says Reïs Hassan triumphantly, pointing in every direction at once. Talhamy tries to show us Medinet Habu and the Memnonium. The Painter vows he can see the heads of the sitting Colossi and the entrance to the Valley of the Tombs of the Kings.

We, meanwhile, stare bewildered, incredulous; seeing none of these things; finding it difficult, indeed, to believe that any one else sees them. The river widens away before us; the flats are green on either side; the mountains are pierced with terraces of rock-cut tombs; while far away inland, apparently on the verge of the desert, we see here a clump of sycamores—yonder a dark hillock—midway between both a confused heap of something that may be either fallen rock or fallen masonry; but nothing that looks like a Temple, nothing to indicate that we are already within recognisable distance of the grandest ruins in the world.

Presently, however, as the boat goes on, a massive, windowless structure which looks (Heaven preserve us!) just like a brand-new fort or prison, towers up above the palm-groves to the left. This, we are told, is one of the propylons of Karnak; while a few whitewashed huts and a little crowd of masts now coming into sight a mile or so higher up, mark the position of Luxor. Then up capers Egendi with his never-failing "Luxor—kharûf—all right!" to fetch down the tar and darabukkeh. The captain claps his hands. A circle is formed on the lower deck. The men, all smiles, strike up their liveliest chorus, and so, with barbaric music and well-filled sails, and flags flying, and green boughs waving overhead, we make our triumphal entry into Luxor.

The top of another pylon; the slender peak of an obelisk; a colonnade of giant pillars half-buried in the soil; the white houses of the English, American, and Prussian Consuls, each with its flagstaff and ensign; a steep slope of sandy shore; a background of mud walls and pigeon-towers; a foreground of native boats and gaily-painted dahabeeyahs lying at anchor—such, as we sweep by, is our first panoramic view of this famous village. A group of turbaned officials sitting in the shade of an arched doorway rise and salute us as we pass. The assembled dahabeeyahs dozing with folded sails, like sea-birds asleep, are roused to spasmodic activity. Flags are lowered; guns are fired; all Luxor is startled from its midday siesta. Then, before the smoke has had time to clear off, up comes the Bagstones in gallant form, whereupon the dahabeeyahs blaze away again as before.

Luxor Temple: Grandeur and Craft, 1844

Prince Puckler-Muskau

The first observation that forced itself upon me, was one that has occurred to many others: viz. how much better the Egyptians understood architecture than we do, and how little we have been able to learn from them. The removal of the second obelisk from here, in order to place it in the centre of the great square of Louis Quinze, at Paris, which was attended with an enormous expense, is no slight proof of this latter assertion. The entrance of the temple at Luxor, is formed by two imposing Pylones of a hundred feet in height; close to the sides of the gate are placed two colosses of forty feet in height, and a few steps from it, and at about double the distance from the colosses to the Pylones, stood the two obelisks, of from eighty to ninety feet in height, one of which has been carried off. This close assemblage of monuments produces a most imposing effect, whilst the same objects dispersed and spread over a large surface, would be completely lost.

The Egyptians never erected an obelisk without a companion, any more than an isolated pillar; but least of all, would they have placed a single obelisk like this in the midst of a large square, where it would only resemble an unmeaning pole, and spoil the appearance of the square, whilst the size of the latter would take away all its importance as a mass, and thus make the great appear artificially small. It is really the greatest pity, that for such an object the noble appearance of the temple entrance was so much weakened, for to destroy it entirely was impossible. The remaining obelisk, formed of the finest pink granite, is in an excellent state of preservation, excepting a trifling damage near the base, on two sides, and the hieroglyphics cut into it two inches deep, are acknowledged to be the most perfect of the kind executed even by the Egyptians. It would, in fact, be impossible to surpass this work, and in the present day it cannot be conceived how they managed to cut into this rocky granite, the most delicate and chastely executed figures with the same precision and facility, as our best sculptors cut into stone. A boy of eleven years of age offered, for the sum of one karie (an Egyptian coin of the value of two and a-half francs) to climb the obelisk by means of these hieroglyphics, and in fact performed this hazardous feat as far as two-thirds of the height, without experiencing the least difficulty; but when he got thus far, he was blown about so violently by the wind, that we promised him two karie, if he would immediately descend.

Life at Thebes, 1850
Florence Nightingale

11 February

Do you want to know how we pass our days, dear people? We rise up early in the morning, and are breakfasted perhaps by eight o'clock. Then we cross the water in the "sandal," which is a small "dingee," to western Thebes; the asses rush into the water to meet us, or the crew carry us ashore: we mount the asses, and with a great multitude—for in Egypt every attendant has his ass, and every ass his attendant—we repair (preceded by a tall man with a spear, his wild turban coming undone in the wind), like a small army, to a tomb. The tomb instantly fills—we suffocate for two or three hours, the guides having, besides, lighted fires and torches therein. When nature can sustain no more, we rush out, and goollehs, bread and dates are laid upon a stone. Those who have strength then begin again, till dark; those who have not, lie on stones in the valley.

Then begins the delightful ride home, the quiet, the silence (except that no Arab is ever silent—the donkey men and the guides talk without one moment's interruption, if it is ten miles or if it is one, the whole way home), the sunset tints, the goats coming home, the women spinning at the head, the gamous (the great Nile buffalo) crossing the little branches of the Nile in large herds on their way home, two little children perhaps riding on the neck of the largest, a stray jackal coming out, and the Pair looking golden in the western sunlight; the evening picture is all beautiful. Our asses enter the river and slide us into the sandal, and home we come to the little fleet of European boats moored under the colonnades of Luxor, which really from the river are almost beautiful.

We dine, and after dinner, when we are all hung up by the tails, like the chameleons, pretending to be dead, and waiting for half-past seven, or at latest eight, to bury us, lo! a dreadful plash of oars, or Paolo puts in his head, with an abominable grin at our mute misery, and says "the Hungarian count!" or "the German professor!" and so on. Mr. B—— immediately retires to his own room, whence he is generally heard to snore. We unwillingly, but nobly, sacrifice ourselves to our duty, sit up (in brown Holland dressing gowns we are sure to have on, having been much too tired to dress), and talk; but we never give one drop of tea, which has greatly limited these visitations, for, in our street, the doors stand always open, and the people have nothing to do but to spend their evenings on board each other's boat. One night, and one night only, we were got out. Capt. ——, good-natured man, came himself in his sandal, and positively carried us off; and one day the —— dined with us, and with all the devotion of Arab hospitality which distinguished us, we killed—was it not beautiful of us?—no, not our horse, we had none, but our dog, for dinner. I think I told you of our dog—a turkey, "as big as donkey," as Paolo said. Oh what a loss was there, how he used to walk majestically up and down the beach in front of the boat, which he believed it his duty to guard, bastinadoing the chickens when they made a noise. He killed two cocks the day he died. No man could get him into a coop (the crew were afraid to go near him), yet he never strayed. No dog ever ventured near our boat while he lived; the moment he was dead, the hungry

Luxor dogs used to come on board every night, till Mustafa, like Cuddie's lady, greeted them with boiling water; and after his death, we never could keep a quail a single night, though our numerous acquaintances kept us well in quails, for our four cats had parties every night, and bared the larder: and we killed him!

As soon as our guests were gone, sometimes before, we went to bed. Don't think us grown quite savage and uncivilised. It is very hard to be all day by the deathbed of the greatest of your race, and to come home and talk about quails or London.

Karnak at Last, 1799

Vivant Denon

Unable, by myself, to take the plan of Karnac temple, or make large views of this mass of ruins, which, at first sight resembles the saw-yard of a quarry, or rather piled mountains, my design was to employ the two hours there in making draughts of the historical low-reliefs. . . .

The day advanced, and the soldiers had not yet obtained anything to eat: travellers are not like Roman heroes, they sometimes feel the want of refreshment: the sun gained upon them, and it was resolved to sleep at Karnac. . . . [Even so, Denon decided that he would need eight days to make a plan 'in the least degree satisfactory.'] I was unable to measure the surface of this group of edifices; but, in encompassing it several times on horseback, at a full trot, I always performed the ride in twenty-five minutes.

[Denon worked on the next day until heat overcame him.] It was so hot that the sun had burned my feet, through my boots; I could remain in one place only by causing my servant to walk between the sun and myself, that the rays might be interrupted, and a little shade thrown upon me by his body; the stones had acquired so much heat, that, in picking up some cornelean agates which are found in great number even within the enclosure of the town, I was so burnt by them, that, in order to carry them, I was obliged to throw them on my handkerchief, as I would have touched hot coals.

Worn out with fatigue, I threw myself down in a little Arabian tomb, which had been prepared for me for the night, and which appeared a delicious chamber, till I was told that, at the time of our passing Karnac before, the throat had there been cut of a Frenchman who had lagged behind the column: the marks of this assassination, still imprinted on the walls filled me with horror; but I was laid down, I was sleepy, and so weary that I believe I should not have risen off the dead body itself of the unfortunate victim.

Dining at Karnak, 1930

Princess Marta Bibescu

Arab musicians sing:

Gardener, give me a rose,

If you give me no rose,

Then a kiss—

A kiss and a bite.

It is light music, but it lasts.

We follow in the night the sandy avenue of sacred rams, that series of 'paternosters.' The perfume of mimosa from the abandoned house of Legrain, a little French dwelling shadowed by the great pylons, comes to us on the Nile breeze. Prince I.D. points out certain lights which move on the pylons up near the stars.

"Your dinner awaits you there," he said.

We went up to the lofty terrace by a half-ruined spiral staircase, like the ones in cathedrals. The handsome serving-men, black shadows against the sky, stood mute and motionless around a small laden table. They must have been jinn out of the air to have carried such a large meal to this place.

At my right, the Nile and mount Assasif with its strawberry and cream tint. At my left, the prodigious ruin of the eighth wonder of the world. The moon hangs high above the table exactly in the center of the four candles enclosed in glass globes. . . .

The Prince has brought a phonograph.

Some American tourists, attracted by the familiar sounds of *Old Man River* in that great solitude, appear, like jacks-in-the-box, at the head of the stairway. The jinn have to drive them away with great flappings of napkins.

When our meal is finished, a jinni who comes to carry out the coffee cups brings me the moon on a silver salver.

Temples on the Other Side, 1819
John Fuller

We reached the plain at a spot several miles to the southward of Gournou and proceeded to the Medinet Abou, which is about equidistant from the mountains and the river. The vast mass of buildings known by that name is so choked up with the ruins of more modern brick structures, that it is difficult to discover its original design.

It is supposed to have composed a royal palace and two temples, the largest of which is the most magnificent to be found in the western division of Thebes. It was approached by two gateways connected by a colonnade on each side, together forming a quadrangle. Within the inner gate is the portico of the temple, on the walls of which is a series of bas-reliefs, representing battles, sieges, and triumphal processions, frightful from the barbarities which they exhibit as practised on the vanquished, but remarkable for the spirit and freedom with which they are executed. They stamp the temple of Medinet Abou as being among the most ancient Egyptian monuments, and as having been constructed while Egypt was still a warlike and conquering nation.

Medinet Habu and the Tombs, 1799

Vivant Denon

I galloped forward to catch some features of the ruins of the temples of Medinet Abu, where the troop would take me up in passing. I arrived an hour before it. I saw that on the right of the temple which adjoins the village there was a square edifice which had been a palace, very small indeed, but to which the neighbouring porticoes would have served for additions, in a climate where galleries of columns and terraces are apartments. This little palace has a character which differs very much from that of all other edifices, both in its plan, in its double storey of square windows, and in a sort of balconies, each of which are sustained by four heads, in the attitude of caryatides. It is to be regretted that this private edifice is in so great a state of destruction, especially in its interior, and that that which remains of its exterior decoration has been so

much injured: the sculptures which decorate the exterior walls, as in that part of the temple of Karnak which I suspect to have been a palace, represent the figures of kings, threatening groups of prostrate captives.

Still going before the troop, and pressed onward by its march, I hastened to the two colossuses, and saw them with the effect of the rising sun, at the hour in which it is customary to go and hear that of Memnon speak: after this, I went to the insulated palace called the *memnonium*.

While I had forgotten to observe, my companions had forgotten to warn me, and I perceived that the detachment had left me half a league in its rear: I galloped to rejoin it. The troop was fatigued, and it has again become a question whether the expedition to the tombs should take place. I swallowed in silence the anger I felt; and I believe that this silence gained more than any words my discontent could have dictated, for, in the end, the route was proceeded on without further discussion. We first crossed the village of Kûrnû, the ancient Necropolis: on approaching these subterraneous abodes, the inhabitants, for the third time, saluted us with several discharges of musketry. This was the only spot in upper Egypt in which it was refused to acknowledge our government; secure in their sepulchral retreats, like larves, they left them only to terrify mankind: guilty of many other crimes, they hid their remorse, and fortified their disobedience, in the obscurity of these excavations, which are so numerous that they alone attest the immense population of ancient Thebes. It was through these humble tombs that the kings were carried two leagues from their palace, into the silent valley that was to become their final dwelling-place: this valley, to the north-east of Thebes, straitens insensibly; flanked by steep mountains, time can have effected but trivial changes in its antique forms, since, toward its extremity, the opening of the rock still scarcely affords space for a passage to the tombs, especially for the sumptuous trains which doubtlessly accompanied ceremonies like these, and which must have produced a striking contrast with the austere asperity of these wild rocks: nevertheless, it is to be believed that this road was taken only for the sake of grander display, for the valley, from its entrance to its end, tending wholly to the south, the point at which are the tombs, can be but a very short distance from the memnonium and yet it was not till after three quarters of an hour's march in this desert that, in the midst of the rocks, we suddenly found the openings, even with the ground. These openings at first present no other architectural ornament than a door, with plain chambranles, of a square form, decorated on the superior part with a flattened oval, on which are inscribed in hieroglyphics a *scarabæus*, a figure of a man having the head of a sparrow-hawk, and, out of the oval, two figures on their knees, in the attitude of adoration: as soon as the sill of the first door is passed, there are found long galleries of twelve feet in width, by twenty in height, lined with stucco, sculptured and painted; the roofs of the vaults, formed in elegant elliptic arches, are covered with hieroglyphics, disposed with so much taste, that, in spite of the uncouthness of their forms, and though there be neither middle-tint nor aerial perspective in these paintings, the ceilings present an agreeable whole, and an assortment of colours of which the effect is rich and grateful.

It would require a stay of some weeks in order to seek and establish a system on the subjects of pictures so numerous, and moreover so mysterious, and I was allowed only a few minutes, and these with a bad grace.

It had been sounded to horse, when I discovered some little chambers, on the walls of which were painted the representations of all sorts of arms, such as maces, coats of mail, tiger-skins, bows, arrows, quivers, pikes, darts, sabres, helmets, goads, and whips; in another, a collection of household utensils, such as cabinets, commodes, chairs, elbow-chairs, stools, and folding mattresses, of an exquisite form, and such as we have these many years admired as the productions of our cabinet-makers, when they have been guided by skilful designers: as painting only copies that which exists, we must suffer ourselves to be convinced that the Egyptians employed indian wood, sculptured and gilt, for their furniture, and brocaded silks for the coverings; to these were added various vessels, as vases, coffee-pots, a ewer, with its salver, a tea-pot, and a basket. Another chamber was devoted to agriculture, and decorated with its implements and labours; as, a plough similar to that used at present, a man sowing grain on the brink of a canal, from the banks of which the inundation has retired, a reaping, performed with the sickle, and rice-fields, in the act of being tilled. In a fourth is a figure in white clothing, playing on a harp of eleven strings; the harp sculptured with ornaments of the same tint and the same wood as those at this moment used by ourselves.

How could I, thus hastily, leave these precious curiosities? I begged with earnestness for a quarter of an hour; and, watch in hand, I was allowed twenty minutes: one person lit the way, while another held a torch to each particular object to which I directed my attention.

Preparing to Collect the 'Young Memnon,' 1817
Giovanni Belzoni

After having taken a cursory view of Luxor and Karnak, to which my curiosity led me on my landing, I crossed the Nile to the west, and proceeding straight to the Memnonium, I had to pass before the two colossal figures in the plain. I need not say, that I was struck with wonder. They are mutilated indeed, but their enormous size strikes the mind with admiration. The next object that met my view was the Memnonium. It stands elevated above the plain, which is annually inundated by the Nile. The water reaches quite to the propylon; and, though this is considerably lower than the temple, I beg leave to observe, that it may be considered as one of the proofs, that the bed of the Nile has risen considerably higher since the Memnonium was erected; for it is not to be supposed that the Egyptians built the propylon, which is the entrance to the temple, so low as not to be able to enter it when the water was at its height. There

are other proofs of this opinion, which I shall have an opportunity of introducing in this volume. The groups of columns of that temple, and the views of the numerous tombs excavated in the high rock behind it, present a strange appearance to the eye. On my approaching these ruins, I was surprised at the sight of the great colossus of Memnon, or Sesostris, or Osymandias, or Phamenoph, or perhaps some other king of Egypt; for such are the various opinions of its origin, and so many names have been given to it, that at last it has no name at all. I can but say, that it must have been one of the most venerated statues of the Egyptians; for it would have required more labour to convey such a mass of granite from Assouan to Thebes, than to transport the obelisk, commonly known under the appellation of Pompey's Pillar, to Alexandria.

As I entered these ruins, my first thought was to examine the colossal bust I had to take away. I found it near the remains of its body and chair, with its face upwards, and apparently smiling on me, at the thought of being taken to England. I must say, that my expectations were exceeded by its beauty, but not by its size.

I observed, that it must have been absolutely the same statue as is mentioned by Norden, lying in his time with its face downwards, which must have been the cause of its preservation. I will not venture to assert who separated the bust from the rest of the body by an explosion, or by whom the bust has been turned face upwards. The place where it lay was nearly in a line with the side of the main gateway into the temple; and, as there is another colossal head near it, there may have been one on each side of the doorway, as they are to be seen at Luxor and Karnak.

To the Valley of the Kings, 1904
William Jarvie

28 January

We rode through a valley which wound about hills and giant rocks for about four miles up to the place known as the 'Tombs of the Kings.' You cannot imagine a more appropriate way to these tombs, for it is truly a way of the dead. Not a tree, not a shrub, not a blade of grass, not even a human being lives in this valley. Yet it is marvellously beautiful in its impressiveness, and the grand tombs at the end are a fitting termination and a most fitting place for the burial of these great men. We went into the tombs of Sethos I, Rameses I, VI and IX, and afterwards had lunch in a tomb, which had been prepared for that purpose.

To the Valley of the Kings, 1938

H.V. Morton

It is a pity that the donkeys that once took you there have almost disappeared, because the slow ride into the Valley of the Dead, the gradual approach to that fiery cleft in the hills, every yard becoming more grim and more desolate, was, I think, a better approach than the rush in a car over a bumpy road.

'Belzoni's Tomb,' 1819
John Fuller

From Gournu a road leads up a ravine in the mountains to an open space surrounded on all sides by steep rocks, in which are excavated the tombs of the Egyptian kings. All of them that have hitherto been discovered are nearly on the same plan. A broad passage leads into one or more lofty saloons which are flanked by smaller chambers, and the walls are richly ornamented with paintings, alluding to the mysterious doctrines and ceremonies of the Egyptian religion, and showing at how early a period the human mind had begun to indulge in speculation as to its future state and destiny.

By far the most interesting of these sepulchres is that called the Tomb of Psammis [Seti I], which had been recently opened by Belzoni, and is fully described in his work. Never having been disposed to the air or wanton injury, the paintings are in perfect preservation, and their colours are as brilliant as the first day they were put on. One apartment appears never to have been finished, as the figures all remain in outline; but this is so fresh, that it seems as if the artist had just quitted his work and was about to return to complete it.

The passage that leads into the tomb slopes downwards, and on the sides there are various groups of figures, among which is distinguished the deceased prince, who appears to be going through various initiatory ceremonies previous to being admitted into the society of the Gods. The passage opens into a vestibule supported by six massive square pillars, where the deities are represented welcoming the hero to their abodes, and Isis is presenting him with the *crux ansata*, the emblem of sovereignty. Within the vestibule is the apartment where the sarcophagus was deposited; a lofty oblong hall with a vaulted ceiling, on which are painted some uncouth figures, supposed to have reference to astronomy.

Walking above the Valley, 1927

Annie Quibell

Most of us feel the need of quietness in the Valley, above all other places, and when often it is very difficult to get it. If one goes with a large party and must stick to them, it is hopeless, but more independent travellers can do better. I would make earnest counsel to make a day of the royal tombs and not to go back for lunch either to Luxor, or over the hill to the rest house at Der el Bahri. People will probably remonstrate and think me mad to stay on after the electric light [in the tombs] is taken off at one o'clock, but by that time we have seen the tombs and want to see the Valley. When the carriages have all clattered down the road and the last of the donkeys has jingled up the slope to Der el Bahri, let us seek out a place under the shadow of a great rock and settle down for an hour or two of peace among the solemn cliffs. There is shade at midday and in the afternoon at the head of the Valley.

After we have rested and filled our souls with the great scene around, there is a choice of ways to return. Down the Valley is the dullest; over the cliff to Der el Bahri is fine and lets us have a beautiful view from the top, but there is a better to be done. There are few good walks in Egypt, but there are some, and perhaps the best of them is the path from Biban el Muluk to Der el Medineh. . . . At the top of the pass are the remains of the shelters where the sentinels of old used to be posted to guard the royal cemetery. From this point onwards the view is glorious. All the line of temples lies below us: Seti's the farthest south, in a clump of palms, Der el Bahri, lying right under the precipice, the Ramesseum, and the big bulk of Medinet Habu to the north. On a desert, in a valley to the right of Medinet Habu are the Tombs of the Queens. On a low desert over the hill of the Sheikh Abd el Gurneh and in the surrounding cliffs, is the cemetery of Thebes, of the nobles and the commonality.

Beyond Medinet Habu, lines on the desert surface show us the palace of Amenhotep III, and the big oblong, just on the edge of the cultivated land, enclosed by high mounds, was once a lake, where he took his pleasure boating. Across the Nile are the temples of Luxor and Karnak and the green country, with three distant peaks closing the prospect.

It is too obvious, perhaps, to say that the more often we can cross to the West Bank the better we shall like it. There is more to see than anywhere else in Egypt and the beauty of the surroundings is so remarkable that every day we spend among them leaves a memory that does not fade in the years.

On the Other Side, 1927

Constance Sitwell

We lingered a little where the Colossi stonily sit, gazing out over the land with strange battered calm, their shadows stretching far over the corn that grows thickly to the very base of their thrones. Not far beyond them is the limit of the irrigated ground, and here we found a camel and an ox yoked together ploughing up the caked soil along the last line of living green. Arid and dusty, the earth flew up behind them. In front of us now was a scorched strip of desert, a stone-strewn waste backed by the tawny precipices of the Libyan mountains, and in that mountain face are the Tombs of the Kings.

It was too hot to hurry the donkeys and slowly we rode us towards the ravine which leads to the tomb where Amenhotep still lies. In the ravine itself the heat and glare grew even more intense. The sun beat down with gathering strength upon the crags of yellow and orange limestone, whose jagged edges quivered above us against the blazing sky. Our narrow path was walled in by ribs of rock which threw out all the heat. At last, in the bare face of the cliff we came to a small door. I thanked heaven, saying to myself that we should find darkness inside; surely, too, inside it would be cool? But I was wrong, for after jumping off our donkeys and leaving the guide behind, we plunged into a yet heavier heat. Deeper we went and deeper into an oven of stone,—down long sloping corridors and down steps, past an empty painted chamber and past a well, then down another stretch of stifling dark until right in the heart of the rock we reached the crypt where the king lies.

The tomb has been lit by electricity, and a harsh light now strikes down on the long-dead face. I looked at it with astonishment; it is wonderful that the mummied flesh, the withered tendons, the brittle bones, should have kept so royal an air. Yes, in spite of time and our desecrations, Amenhotep reposes with kingly calm in his ponderous sarcophagus of sandstone. The silent centuries have come and gone and he has lain alone in the sweltering darkness, suffering no change that seems of any account. How noisily the years have passed by outside, how peacefully for him! No change! Only his stained wrappings have become rags, and some one has put in his folded hands a tiny bunch of flowers that have become skeletons. 'Well,' they made me think, 'flowers were the same, I suppose, in Thebes and Babylon. Poppies in Ninevah and jonquils in Tyre! Solomon saw the bright anemones of Judea growing scarlet and purple amongst the stones; and here are Amenhotep and I each with our little bunch.' I looked at the flagging handful which I still held; the dying fragrance of the clover hung heavily in that stagnant air. Maybe, I thought, as we walked back along the soundless passage, this king liked the honey smell of warm clover too when he was outside in the sun.

On to Aswan

Nile boats now ply this 220-kilometer stretch of the river more than any other, so it is well known to latter-day travelers with its two important towns of Esna and Edfu. The temple at Edfu is easily accessible: Michael Haag describes it as "pure theatre" at which the visitor might cry out:

"Cecil B. de Mille, they have outdone you!" At Kom Ombo the temple of Sobek and Horus stands prominently on high ground overlooking the Nile.

At the end of this stretch of a Nile journey is Aswan—a smiling, lively city. The Nile here seems more sparkling as it flows in a narrower bed created by the islands of the First Cataract—and all day long the white-winged sails of the feluccas speed along its surface.

Upper Egypt in January, 1836
William Ramsay

Edfou, Jan. 9: The fields were looking very beautiful; the system of irrigation is carried on at an immense extent here; it is everything; at every short distance, one sees the water raised from the Nile, by men who hand it up in buckets one to another, into little tanks, till it reaches the top, when it runs down the channels formed for it. There is one great channel which branches off into smaller ones, and these into smaller, till at last it enters the small fields or plots, generally about ten feet square, where it spreads and remains, each little plot being enclosed by raised banks, on which the channels run; when one plot is watered, the entrance for the water is closed with a lump of earth, and the water passes on to the next; when the whole of one division has received its share, the connection with the grand passage is stopped, and so on. The squares are all very carefully kept, and, in fact, in this irrigation consists the whole system of husbandry. A plough, I suppose, is never used; all the land requires is a rough breaking up with a hoe for wheat—for clover not even that. Indian corn is now ripe, and the harvest is going on. It is sown before the rise of the Nile, and is ripe soon after its fall; and it is thus calculated that it must have been the corn which was *not* smitten in the Plagues of Egypt by the hail, as it was sprouting above ground when the other corn, which is sown on the waters retiring, was ripe and fit for the harvest.

The same system seems to be pursued now as in the early and palmy days of this country. The drawings on the walls of some of the tombs display all the processes of husbandry and other daily occupations—and allusions to the Bible might have been made as to what happens at the present day, so much the same has everything remained. It is called "the country that thou waterest with thy foot" and it is so now—the people use their naked feet for stopping the water channels, when required.

A very beautiful plant, which we saw a good deal of today in the fields, is the castor-oil tree—I never saw such a diversity of appearances on one plant at the same time: two totally different flowers on the same stalk, one red, the other white, berries, buds and fruit, something like horse-chestnuts, but more delicate—the young leaves also were of a deep purple, the old ones bright green.

Edfou, 2 Feb. Since we were here last, the appearance of the country is very much altered. The forests of Indian corn are cut down, and the stubble is a poor substitute, especially when the sun is so hot as today; the wheat has grown to eight inches or a foot, in three weeks; the cotton plants have withered, and the irrigation has altered its character.

Raising the Water from the Nile, 1844

Edward Lane

The most important of the occupations which employ the modern Egyptians, and that which engages all but a very small proportion of them, is agriculture.

The great proportion of the cultivable soil is fertilised by the natural annual inundation; but the fields in the vicinity of the river and of the large canals, and some others, in which pits are dug for water, are irrigated by means of machines of different kinds. The most common of these machines is the *shadoof*, which consists of two posts or pillars of wood, or of mud or cane or rushes, about five feet in height, and less than three feet apart, with a horizontal piece of wood extending from top to top, to which is suspended a slender lever, formed by a branch of a tree, having at one end a weight chiefly composed of mud, and at the other, suspended to two long palm-sticks, a vessel in the form of a bowl, made of basketwork, or of a hoop and a piece of woollen stuff or leather; with this vessel the water is thrown up to the height of about eight feet, into a trough hollowed out for its reception. In the southern parts of Upper Egypt, four or five shadoofs are required, when the river is at its lowest, to raise the water to the level of the fields. There are many shadoofs with two levers, etc, which are worked by two men. The operation is extremely laborious.

Another machine much used for the same purpose, and almost the only one employed for the irrigation of gardens in Egypt, is the *sakiyeh*. This mainly consists of a vertical wheel, which raises the water in earthen pots attached by cords, and forming a continuous series; a second vertical wheel, fixed to the same axis, with cogs; and a large, horizontal cogged wheel, which, being turned by a pair of cows or bulls, or a single beast, puts in motion the two former wheels and the pots. The construction of this machine is of a very rude kind; and its motion produces a disagreeable creaking noise.

Edfu, the Ancient Apollinopolis Magna, 1827
The Modern Traveller

At the north-western corner of the village, and on the highest ground, stands a magnificent temple, which, though seen after Dendera, and inferior in size to that of Karnak, is said to yield in effect to neither, the mole and entrance being particularly noble. Numerous brick huts have been erected upon the top of the temple, in the peristyle, and in front of the propylon, so as to render access to it difficult every way. The propylon is in the form of a truncated pyramid, and is at once the most imposing and one of the best proportioned in Egypt. From a base 90 feet in length by 30 feet in width, it rises up on each side of the gateway, 'like two square towers without embrasures,' gradually narrowing till, at the height of 100 feet, it measures on the flattened top only 75 feet by 18. Handsome stairs lead from the gateway on either hand to the different chambers and to the summit. Over the entrance is the globe with the serpent and wings, and on each side is sculptured on the wall a colossal figure of Isis, attended by the hawk-headed deity and another colossal figure armed with a hatchet.

Within the propylon is an open court, or *dromos*, enclosed with high walls covered with sculpture, and adorned with a peristyle of eleven columns, besides five on each side of the doorway, all covered with sculpture. The pronaos, at the northern end of the court, has six columns in front, with varied capitals, resembling the leafs of the *doum*, or Thebaic palm, the leaf of the date-tree, and the budding lotus. The winged globe and serpent occur again over the door, and are frequently repeated on each side, with other strange devices of beetles, long-tailed monkeys, &c. A moulding passes down the corners of the temple, the same as at Dendera and Esneh, so as to include the whole in a frame. Within the pronaos are two rows of columns, three in each row, loaded with hieroglyphics and devices; the globe with wings is painted along the centre of the ceiling, and each intercolumniation has its peculiar ornament; but there is no zodiac. On the walls, Osiris, Isis and Horus are receiving offerings. The entrance to the cella is quite blocked up with sand and rubbish.

Observed at Kom Ombo, 1848

Harriet Martineau

One curious architectural device of the Egyptians, which we found almost everywhere by looking for it, is here apparent at a glance, when one stands on the great circuit wall which encloses the whole group of edifices:—their plan of regularly diminishing the size of the inner chambers, so as to give, from the entrance, an appearance of a longer perspective than exists. They evidently liked an ascending ground, the ascent of which was disguised as much as possible by the use of extremely shallow steps. The roof was made to descend in a great degree, the descent being concealed inside by the large cornices and deep architraves they employed. The sides were made to draw in; and thus the Holy Place was always small; while to those who looked towards it from the outer chambers, (and it was entered by priests alone) it appeared, not small, but distant. I had observed this in some of the Nubian temples, when looking at them sideways from a distance; but here it was particularly evident; the roof descending in deep steps from the portico to the pronaos; from the naos to the corridors; and from the corridors to the adyta, which last were level with the sand.

When I was in the portico, looking up at the architraves, I saw into another ancient secret, which I should have been very sorry to have overlooked. Some of the paintings were half-finished; and their ground was still covered with the intersecting red lines by which the artists secured their proportions. These guiding lines were meant to be effaced as soon as the outlines were completed; yet here they are at the end of, at least, two thousand years! No hand, however light, has touched them, through all the intervening generations of men;—no rains have washed them out, during all the changing seasons that have passed over them;—no damp has moulded them; no curiosity meddled with them. It is as if the artist had lain down for his siesta, his tools beside his hand, and would be up presently to resume his work; yet that artist has been a mummy, lying somewhere in the heart of the neighbouring hills, ever since the time when our island was bristling with forests, and its inhabitants were dressed in skins, and dyed their bodies blue with woad, to look terrible in battle. In another part of the temple, the stone is diced in small squares, to receive the hieroglyphic figures.

Approach to Aswan, 1817

Robert Richardson

We came in sight of the mountain range that bounds the extremity of Egypt towards the south. On the west of the river, the mountain range that had accompanied us all the way from Cairo, destitute of vegetation throughout the whole extent, began to assume a bolder aspect, rising into a round bluff point, overlooking the plain, the town, the ruins of Assuan, the island of Elephantina, the rugged cataract, and the branching Nile. It is called Djibl Howa, or mountain of the wind. Its summit is crowned with the tomb of Sheikh Bass, an honoured Maraboot; halfway down its side are the extensive ruins of the convent of St George, with numerous vaults and excavations, soliciting the attention of the enquiring traveller.

On the east bank of the river the mountain is low, the valley more extended, cultivated and covered with the picturesque palm tree. The aspect gradually ascends in a rocky inclination, and, winding towards the west, terminates at the river, in a precipitous granite cliff, on which stand the ruined walls and houses of the ancient Syene.

Passing the eye along the river as we advance, it was impossible not to be impressed with the singular majesty of its appearance, parted at the bottom of the cataract by the granite base of the green and beautiful island of Elephantina, it poured along its sides as if from an invisible source, and, having joined its divided waters at the low northern end of the island, held on its noble and rapid course to the ocean.

Impressions of Aswan, 1844

Countess Hahn-Hahn

Assuan, Saturday, January 13, 1844: We arrived here yesterday afternoon, having left *Fostat* on 19th December, and remained in *Tentyris* for four-and-twenty hours—thus taking a considerable time for a distance of 105 German miles. In *Europe* such slowness would have driven me to despair: here the voyage is accounted a very favorable one. If we had had contrary winds, it would have lasted a week or fortnight longer. The wind was always in our favour, and very seldom dropped entirely. When it did drop, I must acknowledge that the endless, tiresome towing on the bank, and the thrusting of stakes against the numerous sand-banks, did not very much accelerate our progress. With a favourable wind, in full sail, and under a positive bellowing of joy on the part of the crew, we at length reached *Assuan*, which is very picturesquely situated upon the high eastern bank,—that is to say, the present city—very advantageously concealed behind palm-trees; and the old Arabian city, utterly in ruins, lying upon the fragments of the Roman (as this perhaps upon the Egyptian, the most ancient of all) on a high and rugged hill near the river. The unburnt tiles, with which the Arabs built, and still build, form curious ruinous designs—not common rubbish-heaps, such as are made from burnt tiles and stones, but solitary, disrupted, and prominently standing crags. The walls look as if clawed to pieces by giant hands, or themselves like fixed grey claws, menacing upwards. In the distance, with the transparent back-ground of a beautifully tinted sky, they have a good appearance. Seen near, the material is too paltry; for in this respect you are spoiled in the East, not by what you see of the present, but by what remains of the past. Not far from *Assuan* are the Granite-quarries, which produce the magnificent red granite that in antiquity was so much valued, and received from its home the name of *Syenite*; and upon the small island of *Bidscha*, opposite *Philae*, is found the ten times more beautiful rose-granite, a gateway of which in *Elephantina* is still distinguished as a relic of departed magnificence. The last-named island is opposite to *Assuan*, on this side of the cataracts; the two others lie on the other side of them, about a league up the stream. In the midst of them the *Nile* whirls and curls itself.

Doing Business at Aswan, 1879

Villiers Stuart

On awaking, and taking a bird's eye view from our cabin window of the outer world, a very amusing scene occupied the foreground. A number of Nubian men, women and children were squatting on the sandy shore with their wares arranged on mats before them, patiently awaiting our appearance, smoking and chatting with our crew the while; but no sooner did we step forth, than the greatest excitement prevailed; they started up with one accord and took to brandishing their merchandize over their heads, advertising them by power of lung, and deafening us with a perfect Babel of sounds.

They held out towards us: ostrich eggs, Nubian spears, armlets, necklaces, bracelets, porcupine quills, bows and arrows, ebony clubs, daggers, ostrich feathers, leopard skins, hippopotamus-hide whips, cunningly made baskets, and Egyptian antiquities. Our dragoman took very good care not to let them come on board. Their wares were handed in for our inspection; they themselves were made to keep their distance; and when we went on shore, we landed under escort of a body-guard of our crew, who kept the Nubian merchants off with their sticks.

A little higher up the beach were the goods of a caravan, bound for Khartoum; boxes and bales arranged in a circle formed a sort of camp; their saloon, reception-room, and dining-room was the home of the travellers by day, and their dormitory by night. We visited them at the hour of breakfast; their wants were being ministered to by a number of Nubian girls, some having milk to sell, others cheese, butter, new-baked cakes, cucumbers, buttermilk, and other delicacies. Some were smoking, some were cooking, some were bargaining with the vendors of the eatables; in the middle was a sort of trophy supported on three poles, and consisting of water skins; jars covered with goats' hide with the shaggy hair still on, lanterns, pots, and other camp equipage. Outside the magic circle squatted some camels; it was a very picturesque and amusing scene.

The Brassy Landscape of Nubia, 1927

Constance Sitwell

Some hours later we set out, Jim and I riding in front, Philip following at a little distance behind. We were going up a mountain from which one got a distant view over the brassy landscape of Nubia. It was past noon when at last we reached our goal, a ridge on a craggy cliff facing the south. Arid was the land immediately around us, a confusion of jagged peaks and twisted ravines. It might have all been cast in some heavy metal, so hard and so massive with its surface spread out under a sky hazy with heat.

The Cataract and Nubia

Only by looking at old drawings and photographs, and reading past accounts can we comprehend the change wrought on the landscape by the creation of the two dams at Aswan. The cataract once barred the way to Nubia, and ascending and descending it was a hazardous undertaking. Now, only

by standing on the Aswan Dam (completed in 1902), can one gain some idea of the cataract as it once was: the water swirls round the jagged rocks, it froths but no longer roars.

The Cataract Bars the Way, 1777
Claude Etienne Savary

The cataract is still in our days what is described by Strabo: the rock which bars the middle of the river is bare for six months of the year. Then boats mount and descend by the sides. During the inundation, the waters heaped up between the mountains form one great sheet, and, breaking down every obstacle, spring from eleven feet height. The boats can no longer ascend the stream, and merchandize must be conveyed two leagues over land, above the cataract; they however descend, as usual, and suffer themselves to be plunged into the gulf. They precipitate into it with the rapidity of an arrow, and in an instant are out of sight. They rise again at some distance, when the water becomes calm, to the astonishment of beholders unacquainted with the spectacle; as Seneca beautifully describes it. It is necessary for the boats to be moderately laden, and for the boatmen, who hold by the stern, to be in exact equilibrium, otherwise they would infallibly be swallowed up in the abyss.

Into Nubia, 1897

Sir Arthur Conan Doyle

Between these two huge and barren expanses [of desert], Nubia writhes like a green sandworm along the course of the river. Here and there it disappears altogether, and the Nile runs between black and sun-cracked hills, with the orange drift-sand lying like glaciers in their valleys. Everywhere one sees traces of vanished races and submerged civilisations. Grotesque graves dot the hills or stand up against the skyline: pyramidal graves, tumulus graves, rock graves,—everywhere graves. And, occasionally, as the boats round a rocky point, one sees a deserted city up above,—houses, walls, battlements, with the sun shifting through the empty window squares. Sometimes you learn that it has been Roman, sometimes Egyptian; sometimes all record of its name or origin has been absolutely lost. . . . There they stand, these grim and silent cities, and up on the hills you can see the graves of their people, like the port-holes of a man-of-war. It is through this weird, dead country that the tourists smoke and gossip and flirt as they pass up to the Egyptian frontier.

An Engineer at the Cataract, 1859
Isambard Kingdom Brunel

Philae, February 13, 1859

I now write to you from a charming place; but Assouan, which I left to come here, is also beautiful, and I will speak of that first. It is strange that so little is said in the guide books of the picturesque beauty of these places. Approaching Assouan, you glide through a reef of rocks, large boulders of granite polished by the action of the water charged with sand. You arrive at a charming bay or lake of perfectly still water and studded with those singular jet-black or red-rock islands. In the distance you see a continuation of the river, with distant islands shut in by mountains, of beautiful colours, some a lilac sandstone, some of the bright yellow of the sands of the desert. Above the promontories the water excursions are delicious. You enter at once among the islands of the Cataracts, fantastic forms of granite heaps of boulders split and worn into singular shapes.

After spending a week at Assouan, with a trip by land to Philae, I was so charmed with the appearance of the Cataracts as seen from the shore, and with the deliciously quiet repose of Philae, that I determined to get a boat, and sleep a few nights there. We succeeded in hiring a country boat laden with dates, and emptied her, and fitted up her three cabins. We put our cook and dragoman and provisions, &c., on board, and some men, and went up the Cataract.

It was a most amusing affair, and most beautiful and curious scenery all the way. It is a long rapid of three miles, and perhaps one mile wide, full of rocky islands and isolated rocks. A bird's eye view hardly shows a free passage, and some of the more rapid falls are between rocks not forty feet wide—in appearance not twenty. Although they do not drag the boats up perpendicular falls, of three or four feet, as the travellers' books tell you, they really do drag the boats up rushes of water which, until I had seen it, and had then calculated the power required, I should imprudently have said could not be effected. We were dragged up at one place a gush of water, what might fairly be called a fall of about three feet, the water rushing past very formidably, and between rocks seemingly not more than wide enough to let our boat pass, and this only by some thirty-five men at three or four ropes, the men standing in the water and on the rocks in all directions, shouting, plunging into the water, swimming across the top or bottom of the fall, just as they wanted, then getting under the boat to push it off rocks, all with an immense expenditure of noise and apparent confusion and want of plan, yet on the whole properly and successfully. We were probably twenty or thirty minutes getting up this one, sometimes bumping hard on one rock, sometimes on another, and jammed hard first on one side and then on the other, the boat all the time on the fall with ropes all strained, sometimes going up a foot or two, sometimes losing it, till at last we crept to the top, and sailed quietly on in a perfectly smooth lake. These efforts up the different falls had been going on for nearly eight hours and the relief from noise was delicious. We selected a quiet spot under the temples of Philae.

The Rush of the Cataract, 1836

Lord Lindsay

The cry rose that we were going down the stream again! I sprung out, the vessel was edging away from the rock—I leapt and caught by my hands, my feet in the water; the Arabs pulled me up, and I was safe, thank God! Twice did the boat nearly escape us, the current was so violent; at last we got her safely lashed to the rock with all the ropes we had, and for an hour, or more, the men were occupied in landing everything portable: first our things, then the oars, planks, &c., of the boat, lastly their own stores of dates and biscuits, which they could not touch (honest fellows!) till ours were safe. We expected every minute to see the ropes break and the boat topple over, lying sideways as she did, the deck half under water.

Here we were then, and a most extraordinary scene it was to be in! Wild and picturesque at all times, doubly so now, dark purple clouds lowering around us, rain pouring (a wonder of itself in Upper Egypt), lightning flashing, and thunder outroaring the rapids that were dashing past on either side of our islet, covered as it was with boxes, books, pipes, guns, crockery, pigeons, fowls, lambs, goats, and last but not least, two chameleons, poor things!

Philae, 1825

R.R. Madden

There are four recollections of a traveller which might tempt him to live forever: the sea view of Constantinople, the sight of the Coliseum by moonlight, the prospect from the summit of Vesuvius by dawn, and the first glimpse of Philae at sunset.

Philae, 1852

Arthur Penrhyn Stanley

And now, it is immediately above the roar of these rapids—but still in the very centre of these colossal rockeries—that emerges into sight an island lying in the river—fringed with palms, and crowned with a long line of temples and colonnades. This is Philae.

The Island of Philae, 1833

Robert Curzon

Excepting the Pyramids, nothing in Egypt struck me so much as when on a bright moonlit night I first entered the court of the great temple of Philae. The colours of the paintings on the walls are as vivid in many places as they were the day they were finished: the silence and the solemn grandeur of the immense buildings around me were most imposing; and on emerging from the lofty gateway between the two towers of the propylon, as I wandered

about the island, the tufts of palms, which are here of great height, with their weeping branches, seemed to be mourning over the desolation of the stately palaces and temples to which in ancient times all the illustrious of Egypt were wont to resort, and into whose inner recesses none might penetrate; for the secret and awful mysteries of the worship of Osiris were not to be revealed, nor were they even to be spoken of by those who were not initiated into the highest orders of the priesthood. Now all may wander where they choose, and speculate on the uses of the dark chambers hidden in the thickness of the walls, and trace out the plans of the courts and temples with the long lines of columns which formed the avenue of approach from the principal landing-place to the front of the great temple.

I have been three times at Philae, and indeed I had so great an admiration of the place, that on my last visit, thinking it probable that I should never again behold its wonderful ruins and extraordinary scenery, I determined to spend the day there alone, that I might meditate at my leisure, and wander as I chose from one well-remembered spot to another, without the incumbrance of half a dozen people staring at whatever I looked at, and following me about out of pure idleness. Greatly did I enjoy my solitary day, and whilst leaning over the parapet on the top of the great Propylon, or seated on one of the terraces which overhung the Nile, I in imagination repeopled the scene with the forms of the priests and worshippers of other days, restored the fallen temples to their former glory, and could almost think I saw the processions winding round their walls, and heard the trumpets, and the harps, and the sacred hymns in honour of the great Osiris. In the evening a native came over with a little boat to take me off the island, and I quitted with regret this strange and interesting region.

Reaching Derr, 1817

Giovanni Belzoni

A few miles above this place the Nile turns towards the north-west, and as the wind blew mostly from that quarter, we had it right against us, besides a very strong current, for the Nile was nearly at its height. Though the day was very hot, the night was exceedingly cold, considering the climate we were in. At this place we found it very difficult to advance, for the wind still continued strong ahead, and the sailors could not track the boat by ropes on the shore, as the bank was covered with thorns and acacia trees, so that it took us two days to reach the territory of Derr, where the river resumes its course again to the south. From the trees I have mentioned we gathered a little gum-arabic; and the reis of the boat caught some chameleons, which we intended to keep alive.

Entering the Temple at Abu Simbel, 1817

Giovanni Finati

We availed ourselves of such implements and contrivances as seemed adapted to facilitate the labour, and as soon as some appearance of the great architrave of a portal came to light, trunks of the palm-trees were driven down as piles, at the distance of two or three yards from it, which bore the loose mass from behind, and enabled us to scoop out a sort of well in front of them, which we consolidated, from time to time, by the pouring of water.

After three weeks . . . a corner of the doorway itself became visible. . . . At that very moment, while the fresh clamours and new disputes were going on with our crew, and the attention of all distracted, I, being one of the slenderest of the party, without a word, crept through into the interior, and was thus the first that entered it, perhaps for a thousand years.

Unlike all the other grottoes in Egypt and Nubia, its atmosphere, instead of presenting a refreshing coolness, was a hot and moist vapour, not unlike that of a Turkish bath, and so penetrating that paper, carried within, soon became as saturated as if it had been dropped in the river. It was, however, a consoling and almost an unexpected circumstance, that the run of sand extended but a little way within the aperture, and the remainder of the chambers were all unencumbered.

The Great Temple at Abu Simbel, 1817

Charles Irby and James Mangles

We now entered the temple, and thus ended all our labours, doubts and anxiety. This morning we built a wall to barricade the door; it was made of stones and mud, with a foundation of date trees driven in to prevent the sand from giving way. A toad crept out of the temple while we were thus employed, and hid himself in the rubbish at the entrance. We now brought down to the boat some statues of calcarious stone which we found in the temple. . . . At three we went to work again; two of the Ebsambal peasants came, and appeared astonished that we succeeded. They said the country people had no idea we should have accomplished our undertaking. They appeared to think

the temple would make a good hiding place for their cattle, &c., whenever the Bedouins came to rob them.

At the Second Cataract, 1927

Constance Sitwell

The naked black boys run panting across the sand and up the slope toward us. They have been swimming and shooting the rapids of the second cataract, and now, having each been given a coin, they fling themselves down for a rest.

I, too, lie outstretched in a patch of shade on the top of a great rock that stands high above the surrounding country. Jim and Philip, their eyes shut, are resting in the shadow of another ledge. We made our start many hours ago, at break of dawn, to avoid the heat of the day. For part of the way our boatman rowed, and sometimes they had to tow the boat along, but there were spells when they could sit and sing while the boat beat its way up the river under sail. At last we reached these curious rocks sticking up out of the broad flood that swirls around them—black rocks, rounded and glistening like gigantic lumps of coal.

From my place here I can see our boat tied up to the bank far below; it is gaily bedecked with flags, and at the top of the mast one long pennon with the star and crescent hangs limp in the lifeless air. On deck lies a dog, asleep, with lolling tongue. As far as I can see the Nubian crew, squatting on the shore, are still as busy as ever talking. Their voices do not reach me, but I can see their gesticulations. So dead black is their skin that they look as if they had been rubbed over with blacklead and then polished like a grate; their hair is glistening with castor oil. They talk and talk, but here there is silence except for the far-off sound of the water rushing, leaping and dashing amongst the rocks.

I have to shut my eyes at last because of the glare, and when I open them again it is to watch a beetle crawling over the glittering flakes of stone. It is a shiny and fantastic creature with glassy wings and a silver body spotted with bronze. It moves slowly among a host of ants that are hurrying in and out between the hot boulders. Idly I look at them and their settlement full of stirs; ant jostles ant in the narrow ways, and they are all black—as black as those Nubian boatmen down below. Here is a city of

Ethiopians—a miniature city that with one brush of my hand I could sweep way. Ethiopia! How rich and hot the name sounds; but it tells of a glory which is fled. . . .

Ethiopia lies there before me; on one side of the Nile its sand is ashen grey, on the other a tawny gold. And this terrible waterless desert stretches away eastward to the coast; beyond there heaves the Red Sea. Southward and eastward it shimmers in the heat-haze, and somewhere beyond the horizon there roam dapple giraffes—fairy-tale creatures with velvety skins and liquid eyes. I wonder, are they frightened of the lions? The Kings of Ethiopia used to hunt with lions. . . . Kings with lions at their side! Ethiopia, once great, your glory has indeed been swept away! Where are the emeralds and the gold, where are the gums, and resins, and fragrant woods that once you poured forth? How long ago is it since travelling companies of tall merchantmen brought their riches to Egypt over these blazing sands—their white ivory, white wool and white ostrich plumes, their ebony and slaves like ebony. Bunched feathers of bright colours, and small bewildered Negro boys were offered to the great ladies of Thebes and Heliopolis.

The Great Rock at Abu Sir, 1836

Lord Lindsay

Our sailors, full of fun and merriment, punted and rowed us up the river, as far as the boat could ascend, and then, landing on the western bank, we proceeded on foot, alternately over sand and rock, to Abousir, a lofty cliff that overhangs the rapids, conspicuous from afar, and covered, we found, with the names of former travellers.

Climbing the rock, the Nile lay before us like the map of an Archipelago—so it seemed to me at first, till the eye presently discovered the main stream of the river winding between myriads of little black islets, tufted with Egyptian acacia, and glistening in the sunbeams like those at Philæ—themselves washed by hundreds of collateral streamlets that glitter, foam and roar in emulation of their parent. Ten miles in length, and two in breadth, are these rapids. It is the lower cataract (that above Assuan) on an infinitely larger scale, but the impressions excited are widely different; there you feel an interest in every rock as you pass it, you admire their savage grandeur individually, and the rapids the while are dashing away under your feet—there you thread a labyrinth—here you look down on one, quite bewildered.

The prospect, miles to the eastward, is bounded by the prolongation of Gebel Mokkatam—to the south, by the mountains of Dongola—it was something to have seen them! It was a sad thought, that I had reached the limits of my southern excursion; sad—though now every step I took would bring me nearer to my happy family homes in England and Scotland! From one of the western crags I had a partial view over the Libyan desert—a dreary sight. While William carved our names in the rock, where many a future traveller will read them in association with those of Belzoni, Burckhardt, Irby and Mangles, &c. I enjoyed half an hour's delightful rumination, on a most commodious natural seat that overhangs the Nile beyond the rock Abousir, and on which before departure, I cut my cipher by way of claiming it as my own. . . . Nowhere else have we attempted to immortalize ourselves in this way.

The Writers

88, 127 **Giovanni Belzoni** (1778–1823). Born in Padua, Belzoni—showman, engineer, traveler, archaeologist—went to Egypt in 1815, where he was employed by the British Consul General to collect and explore antiquities. He collected the statue of Ramesses II now in the British Museum, excavated the great temple at Abu Simbel, and opened the tomb of Seti I.

80 **Princess Marta Bibescu** (1888–1973), daughter and wife of Romanian aristocrats, was an outstanding writer. Her rare beauty consistently led men to fall in love with her. In Egypt in 1930, she wrote brief observations of her experiences.

Isambard Kingdom Brunel (1806–59). It is little known that Britain's two greatest engineers met in Cairo at Christmas in the last year of both their lives. Robert Stephenson was a frequent visitor to Egypt to supervise the building of the railway between Alexandria and Cairo; Brunel visited only once, with his family, for the sake of his health, and took great pleasure in what was for him an unusual period of leisure. *120*

James Silk Buckingham (1786–1855) went to sea as a boy, traveled widely in the Mediterranean including Egypt, left the sea to become a journalist and newspaper editor, and was elected to the reformed Parliament 1832–37. He wrote about his Levant travels, but it was not until 1855 in his Autobiography that he wrote of Egypt. *55*

Mrs. M. Carey (fl. 1850) traveled up the Nile on a four-month winter cruise in 1863–64, in the company of a disabled, elderly male cousin, his manservant, Selina his delicate daughter, and a maid. She illustrated the resulting book on her journey with some lively pictures. *53*

2 **John Carne** (1789–1844) traveled in the East in 1821 and returned to be ordained as a deacon and live quietly in the west of England. There he recorded his travels, wrote a book about Syria and the Holy Land illustrated by W.H. Bartlett, and several biographies of missionaries.

60 **Jean François Champollion** (1790–1832) received credit for deciphering the hieroglyphs. Born at Figeac in France, he studied Oriental languages and taught in universities, eventually becoming professor of Egyptian language and archaeology. It was not until 1828 that he first visited Egypt.

47, 125 **Robert Curzon** (1810–73) was a British Member of Parliament who traveled in the Middle East to seek out and purchase ancient manuscripts in monastery libraries. In 1841 he became private secretary to the British Ambassador in Constantinople, and later Joint Commissioner with Russia defining the Persian–Turkish border.

Baron Dominique Vivant Denon (1747–1825) joined the French diplomatic service, and later Napoleon's Commission to Egypt. With General Desaix he traveled on the Nile, recording antiquities. Later, in France, he became Director of the Central Museum of Art, and in 1804, Director General of Museums. *77, 82*

Sir Arthur Conan Doyle (1859–1930), creator of the legendary detective Sherlock Holmes, trained as a doctor, but gave up practice for a full-time writing career. After his visit to Egypt he wrote the novel *The Tragedy on the Korosko* (1897), about a disastrous Nile tour. *119*

Lady Lucie Duff Gordon (1821–69), suffering from tuberculosis, and unable to live in the English climate, settled in Egypt, mainly in Luxor, in 1862. Her vivid letters were published and brought her fame. Other travelers viewed her with as much reverence as the temples they visited, but it was the Egyptians who truly loved her: "The great lady who was just and had a heart that loved the Arabs." *21*

2, 7, 41 **Abu al-Kasim Mohammed bin Ali al-Museli Ebn Haukal** (tenth century), trader, adventurer, and geographer, was born in Baghdad and traveled for thirty years in the Islamic world and Europe. Well acquainted with the literature of his predecessors, he based his book (completed c. 977) as much on his own observations as on those of other writers.

8, 14, 30, 67 **Amelia B. Edwards** (1831–92) wrote for journals and published novels and travel books. Shocked by wanton destruction of the monuments of Egypt, she funded scientific excavations and founded the Egypt Exploration Fund in 1882 (now the Egypt Exploration Society), which still finances archaeology in Egypt.

128 **Giovanni Finati** (1787– c.1829), an Italian recruited to the French army, deserted to the Turks and served in Muhammad 'Ali's army. He acted as dragoman/janissary to the British Consulate, accompanying W.J. Bankes, who edited his memoirs, and other British travelers around Egypt and the Near East. He eventually visited Britain, and later established a hotel in Cairo.

John Fuller (fl. 1820), an Englishman, traveled through the East in 1818–19 and displayed a quiet, accurate sense of the places he sensitively observed. *8, 81, 93*

Countess Ida Hahn-Hahn (1805–80), German aristocrat and novelist, traveled in the Near East after her divorce, with a male partner, in the mid-1840s. She converted to Catholicism in 1850, established a convent in Germany, and lived there for the rest of her days. *112*

Robert Hay (1799–1863) lived in Egypt in 1823–24, studying and recording both ancient and Islamic monuments. He published *Illustrations of Cairo* in 1840. He also made plaster casts of the monuments, now in the British Museum. His vast records are preserved in the British Library. *42*

Ibn Jubayr (1145–1217), son of an Arab family from Valencia, worked as secretary to the governor of Granada. In 1183 he went to Mecca, keeping a daily record of two years' travel. He traveled the Nile and crossed the desert to the Red Sea. *62*

44, 66, 129 **Captain Charles Leonard Irby** (1789–1845), resigning his naval commission in 1816, set off with James Mangles to tour Europe. The journey developed far beyond their original design and they ended up assisting Belzoni in opening the temple at Abu Simbel.

91 **William Jarvie** (1841–1921), a New York dentist from 1872 to 1916, accompanied his brother and sister on a long holiday in the Middle East in 1903. The letters he wrote home were printed for family members.

104 **Edward Lane** (1801–76) learned classical and vernacular Arabic before moving to Egypt in 1825, where he chose to live as an Egyptian, apart from other foreigners. He traveled widely and studied ancient, modern, and Islamic Egypt. His Arabic-English *Lexicon* (1877) is still a great authority and his *Description of Egypt* was finally published in 2000 in Cairo.

123, 134 **Lord Lindsay (Alexander William Crawford)** (1812–80) inherited the title of twenty-fifth Earl of Crawford.

He traveled in Egypt and Palestine in 1836–37 with William Ramsay, and published an account of their travels in 1838.

Pierre Loti (1850–1923) traveled widely as a French naval officer, and later became a novelist and travel writer, memorializing the places to which he had journeyed. He created an extraordinary house (now a museum) in his birth place of Rochefort in northern France. *3*

Dr. Richard R. Madden (1798–1886) was an Irish doctor who traveled in Egypt in 1825 and 1840. In 1825 he became physician to Consul General Henry Salt, and attended him when he died. He went on to various appointments concerned with bringing slaves and other peoples, including the Irish, to independence. *3, 124*

Captain James Mangles (1786–1867) was a naval officer who, with his friend Charles Irby, traveled in the East in 1817–18. *44, 66, 129*

24 **Deborah Manley** (1932–) was born in England but lived in India and Canada for most of her early life. She later lived in Nigeria, before returning to England in 1960 to work in publishing for Africa. She has put together a number of anthologies on various places that interest her—mainly Egypt.

50, 108 **Harriet Martineau** (1802–76) suffered from "feeble health and deafness," though neither stopped her from publishing political and feminist articles, consulting cabinet ministers, and traveling in America. In 1848 she set off to explore Egypt and Palestine, a journey she recorded in three volumes.

38 **George Melly** (fl. 1850), son of a Liverpool merchant, traveled as far as Khartoum with his family in 1850–51. They returned across the desert via Korosko, but sadly his father died on the journey and is buried in the village cemetery at Gagee.

H.V. Morton (c. 1890–1975) was a journalist. His *In Search of . . .* books appeared from 1927 to within a few years of his death, and have seldom been out of print. His *In the Steps of the Master* appeared first in 1939, and his *Middle East* in 1941. *92*

Florence Nightingale (1820–1910), founder of modern nursing, had little experience of nursing before visiting Egypt. In the Crimean War she was invited to take nurses to Scutari, accompanied by the Bracebridges, with whom she traveled in Egypt. She worked for the next fifty years to improve health in the British Army and in Britain. *17, 32, 74*

Sophia Poole (1804–91), sister of the Arabist Edward Lane, lived with her two sons in Egypt for seven years. In 1844–46, she published a study of the life of Egyptian women, *The Englishwoman in Egypt* (republished in 2003). In England, she collaborated with her younger son on photographic books of the Middle East. *13*

71 **Prince Hermann Ludwig Heinrich Puckler-Muskau** (1785–1871), an aristocrat with estates in eastern Germany, traveled in Egypt and Sudan in 1837. His account was translated into English in 1845.

95 **Annie Quibell** (1862–1927), excavator and draftswoman, worked with Flinders Petrie and married archaeologist James Quibell, who was Keeper of the Egyptian Museum (1913–23) and Secretary-General of the Egyptian Antiquities Department (1923–25).

101 **William Ramsay** (fl. 1830s) was a Scotsman who traveled with Lord Lindsay in the Middle East. He died shortly after their trip and entries from his diary were added to Lindsay's account.

110 **Dr. Robert Richardson** (1779–1847) was physician to Lord Belmore for his two-year tour of the Eastern Mediterranean. His *Travels* (1822) are observant and thoughtful. Byron remarked in a letter to Lady Blessington: "The author is just the sort of man I should like to have with me in Greece—clever both as a man and a physician."

Claude Etienne Savary (1750–88) was a French traveler who visited Egypt 1776–79, to study the manners and monuments, and later wrote about the country using previous travelers' records as sources. He translated the Qur'an (1781), wrote a life of Muhammad (1783), and an Arabic grammar, published posthumously in 1789. *118*

Constance Sitwell (1888–1974), daughter of a tea planter, lived the life of the Edwardian gentry: London 'seasons,' summers in Scotland, and travels with her parents. She went to Egypt twice, evoking the country beautifully in two books. *97, 116, 131*

Dean Arthur Penrhyn Stanley (1815–81) became Regius Professor of Ecclesiastical History at Oxford in 1856, the year he visited Egypt. He was Dean of Westminster from 1864 until his death. *124*

27, 35, 57 **John Lloyd Stephens** (1805–52), an American lawyer, went to Europe for his health. His tour extended to Greece, Turkey, Russia, and in 1836, Egypt. He met others with an interest in archaeology, and traveled to Sinai, Petra, and the Holy Land, returning home to write *Incidents of Travel* (1837). From 1839, he explored Central America and the Yucatan, with which his name is most linked.

114 **Villiers Stuart** (1827–95), an ordained minister, gave up holy orders to enter politics. He was attached to the mission of reconstruction of Egypt in 1883, and commissioned to investigate the condition of the country.

39, 48 **Eliot Warburton** (1810–52), a lifelong friend of Kinglake, gave up a law career to travel and write. In 1843 he toured Syria, Palestine, and Egypt, and wrote *The Crescent and the Cross* (1844), which went into seventeen editions. In 1852, traveling to South America, his steamer caught fire and he perished.

Cuthbert Young (fl. 1850), from North Shields, near Newcastle, wrote his *Wayfarer's Notes* following his journey in 1846–47 with two purposes in mind: to sketch the religious features of some countries and to add to the descriptions of the Egyptian monuments. *66*

Bibliography

Belzoni, Giovanni, *Narrative of the Operations and Recent Discoveries in Egypt and Nubia*, John Murray, London, 1820.

Bibescu, Marta, *Egyptian Day*, Harcourt Brace, New York, 1930.

Brunel, Isambard, *The Life of Isambard Kingdom Brunel, Civil Engineer*, Longmans, Green, and Co., London, 1870.

Buckingham, James Silk, *Autobiography of James Silk Buckingham, including his voyages, travels, adventures, speculations, successes and failures, faithfully and frankly related,* Longman, Brown, Green, London, 1855.

Carey, M.L.M., *Four months in a dahabeeh, or narrative of a winter's cruise on the Nile*, Booth, London, 1863.

Carne, John, *Letters from the East,* Henry Colburn, London, 1826.

Champollion, Jean-François, *Letters Written during His Voyage to Egypt in 1828–9,* Paris, 1829.

Conan Doyle, Sir Arthur, *The Tragedy of the Korosko,* London, 1897; republished by Hesperus Press, London, 2003.

Curzon, Robert, *Visits to Monasteries in the Levant*, Arthur Baker, London, 1855.

Denon, Vivant, *Travels in Upper and Lower Egypt during the Campaign of General Bonaparte,* translated by E.A. Kendal, London, 1802; reissued by Darf Publishers Ltd., London, 1986.

Duff Gordon, Lucie, *Letters from Egypt,* Macmillan, London, 1875.
Ebn Haukal, *The Oriental Geography of Ebn Haukal, an Arabian Traveller of the Tenth Century,* translated by Sir William Ousely, London, 1800.
Edwards, Amelia, *One Thousand Miles up the Nile,* Longmans Green, London, 1877.
Finati, Giovanni, *Narrative of the Life and Adventures of Giovanni Finati,* John Murray, London, 1830.
Fuller, John, *Narrative of a Tour through Some Parts of the Turkish Empire,* John Murray, London, 1829.
Hahn-Hahn, Ida Marie, *Letters from the Orient, or Travels in Turkey, Egypt and the Holy Land,* Colburn, London, 1845.
Ibn Jubayr, *The Travels of Ibn Jubayr,* translated by R.J.C. Broadhurst, Jonathan Cape, London, 1952.
Irby, Charles Leonard and James Mangles, *Travels in Egypt and Nubia, Syria and Asia Minor; during the years 1817 & 1818,* London, 1823.
Jarvie, William, *Letters Home from Egypt and Palestine,* New York, 1904.
Lane, Edward William, *Manners and Customs of the Modern Egyptians,* Charles Knight, London, 1837; The American University in Cairo Press, Cairo and New York, 2003.
Lindsay, Lord, *Letters from Egypt, Edom and the Holy Land, (including notes of William Ramsay),* Henry Colburn, London, 1838.
Loti, Pierre, *Egypt,* T. Werner Laurie, London, 1910.
Madden, Dr. R.R., *Travels in Turkey, Egypt, Nubia and Palestine,* Whittaker, Treacher and Co., London, 1829.
Martineau, Harriet, *Eastern Life, Past and Present,* Lea and Blanchard, Philadelphia, 1848.
Melly, George, *Khartoum and the Blue and White Niles,* Colburn and Co., London, 1851.

Modern Traveller II: Egypt, Nubia and Abyssinia, Oliver and Boyd, Edinburgh, 1827.

Morton, H.V., *Through Lands of the Bible,* Methuen, London, 1938.

Nightingale, Florence, *Letters from Egypt: A Journey on the Nile,* ed. Anthony Sattin, Weidenfeld and Nicolson, New York, 1987.

Poole, Sophia, *The Englishwoman in Egypt,* Charles Knight, London, 1844; The American University in Cairo Press, Cairo and New York, 2003.

Puckler-Muskau, Prince Hermann, *Egypt and Mehemet Ali,* Henry Colburn, London, 1845.

Quibell, Annie, *A Wayfarer in Egypt,* Methuen, London, 1925.

Ramsay, William (*see* Lindsay).

Richardson, Dr. Robert, *Travels along the Mediterranean and Parts Adjacent in Company with the Earl of Belmore,* T. Cadell, London, 1822.

Savary, Claude Etienne, *Letters on Egypt,* P. Byrne, Dublin, 1787.

Sitwell, Constance, *Lotus and Pyramid,* Jonathan Cape, London, 1927.

Stanley, Dean Arthur Penrhyn, *Sinai and Palestine,* John Murray, London, 1856.

Stephens, John Lloyd, *Incidents of Travel in Egypt, Arabia Petraea and the Holy Land,* Ward, London, 1876.

Stuart, Villiers, *Nile Gleanings,* John Murray, London, 1879.

Warburton, Eliot, *The Crescent and the Cross,* Hurst and Blackett, London, 1845.

Young, Cuthbert, *A Wayfarer's Notes on the Shores of the Levant, and the Valley of the Nile . . .,* W.P. Kennedy, Edinburgh, 1848.